HM TREASURY

 **Cabinet**Office

The future role of the third sector in social and economic regeneration:

final report

July 2007

Cm 7189

£18.00

HM Treasury contacts

This document can be found on the Treasury website at:

hm-treasury.gov.uk

For general enquiries about HM Treasury and its work, contact:

Correspondence and Enquiry Unit
HM Treasury
1 Horse Guards Road
London
SW1A 2HQ

Tel: 020 7270 4558
Fax: 020 7270 4861
E-mail: ceu.enquiries@hm-treasury.gov.uk

Printed on at least 75% recycled paper.
When you have finished with it please recycle it again.

ISBN 978-0-10-171892-9
PU245

CONTENTS

FOREWORD BY THE PRIME MINISTER - THE THIRD SECTOR AT THE HEART OF SOCIETY

I believe that there is no problem in this country that can't be solved by the people of this country. Millions of people choose to bring about social change and to solve the problems we face through the third sector. In every part of our society voluntary organisations, community groups and social enterprises are making people's lives better, are fighting inequality and are creating a better environment for us to live in.

I believe that a successful modern democracy needs at its heart a thriving and diverse third sector. Government cannot and must not stifle or control the thousands of organisations and millions of people that make up this sector. Instead, we must create the space and opportunity for it to flourish, we must be good partners when we work together and we must listen and respond. This is what we set out in this review. A vision of how the state and the third sector working together at all levels and as equal partners can bring about real change in our country.

In preparing this review, we have listened to and learnt from thousands of organisations from all over England. These contributions have helped us build a clear understanding about how we as Government can create the right support that individuals and local groups need from Government. We will invest over £500 million through the Office of the Third Sector over the 2007 CSR years to make this vision a reality.

At the heart of our approach is our desire to support those thousands of small community organisations who play such a vital role our society. We want them to be free to access the funding or advice they need in a way that suits them. We are investing in small grant schemes and endowing communities to allow local people to make decisions locally about how their groups can build communities and change lives.

To complement this support we are making it clear in this report how much we value the role of the sector in campaigning for social change and giving a voice to the most vulnerable members of society.

The third sector is also helping to change the way we think about business. Thousands of social enterprises are changing the decisions we make as consumers and delivering social and environmental outcomes using business approaches.

This review also signals our continuing support for a range of issues from youth volunteering and giving to mentoring and befriending. It sets out new areas of work to support the skills of those who work and volunteer in the sector and how we will work with the sector to create a real understanding of the value it brings to our country.

Together these measures set out a new framework for a growing partnership between the third sector and Government. It is a relationship that will go from strength to strength as we build a stronger and fairer country.

Gordon Brown

INTRODUCTION

1.1 The third sector[1] is a vital component of a fair and enterprising society, where individuals and communities feel empowered and enabled to achieve change and to meet social and environmental needs. The Government recognises the value of the diversity of organisations in the sector in providing voice for underrepresented groups, in campaigning for change, in creating strong, active and connected communities, in promoting enterprising solutions to social and environmental challenges and in transforming the delivery and design of public services. The third sector has always been at the heart of social and environmental change and the Government wants to continue to work to create the conditions where organisations can grow and achieve their aims.

THE THIRD SECTOR REVIEW

2007 Comprehensive Spending Review

1.2 Budget 2006 announced that the 2007 Comprehensive Spending Review (2007 CSR) would be informed by a review into the future role of the third sector in social and economic regeneration. The 2007 CSR will set departmental spending plans and priorities for the years 2008-09, 2009-10 and 2010-11, within the overall spending limits set at Budget 2007. Budget 2007 confirmed that current spending will increase by an average of 1.9 per cent per year in real terms over the 2007 CSR years with net investment rising to 2 ¼ per cent of GDP. This increase in overall resources, alongside savings released by the value for money programme, will enable Government to sustain the pace of investment in frontline services, focus additional investment on key priorities and respond to the long-term challenges and opportunities that will transform both the environment in which public services operate and the UK's role in the world.

1.3 The third sector review, is one of a series of detailed policy reviews informing the 2007 CSR and the Government's response to the long-term challenges of demographic and socio-economic change, the intensification of cross border competition, acceleration in the pace of innovation and technical diffusion, continued global uncertainty and poverty, and increasing pressure on our natural resources and the global climate.[2] The third sector review is run jointly by HM Treasury and the Cabinet Office and is overseen by a cross-departmental ministerial group and advised by a third sector advisory panel, drawn from organisations across the third sector.

The consultation

1.4 Budget 2006 announced that the review would be informed by the largest ever consultation the Government had held with the third sector, reaching all parts of England and listening to all parts of the sector. The first stage of open consultation from May 2006 to November 2006 reached over 1,000 organisations through 93 consultation events, held in partnership with Government Offices, Government departments, and national, regional and local third sector networks and organisations. Amongst these events were specific events with corporates, social enterprises, credit unions, mutuals and cooperatives, young people's organisations, faith groups, lesbian, gay, bisexual and

---

[1] The Government defines the third sector as non-governmental organisations that are value-driven and which principally reinvest their surpluses to further social, environmental or cultural objectives. It includes voluntary and community organisations, charities, social enterprises, cooperatives and mutuals.

[2] Long-term opportunities and challenges for the UK analysis for the 2007 CSR, HM Treasury, November 2006.

transgender communities and other equalities groups.[3] During the first stage of consultation, over 250 written responses were also received from a wide range of organisations.

Box 1.1 Diversity in the third sector

The Government defines the third sector as non-governmental organisations that are value-driven and which principally reinvest their surpluses to further social, environmental or cultural objectives. There is a wide diversity of organisations however that make up the third sector and it is critical that relationship between the Government and the third sector reflects this diversity. The sector can be most simply categorised as follows:[4]

Voluntary and community organisations (VCOs), consisting of charities (registered and unregistered) and of non-charitable VCOs - in England and Wales at the end of 2006 there were 168,600 registered charities (not including 21,800 subsidiary charities). They range from household names such as Barnardo's (one of the 630 registered charities with annual income over £10 million) to the small trust founded to relieve hardship in a specific parish (typical of the 35,300 registered charities with annual income under £1,000). A recent estimate suggests there are around 110,000 unregistered charities. Unregistered charities include universities, many national museums and galleries, some housing associations, and numerous small educational and religious bodies.

Information about non-charitable VCOs is scarce as many of them operate unknown either to public bodies or to researchers. Their variety in size and activities is broadly the same as for charities, though they also include some types of organisations - such as Community Amateur Sports Clubs, and bodies with what the law treats as a political purpose (e.g. Amnesty International) – that are outside the scope of charity. In common to organisations in this category is that they exist and operate for an altruistic purpose rather than for private benefit; that they were set up, and could be wound up, without needing the permission of the state; and that they rely to a greater or lesser extent on volunteers.

Social enterprises – in 2005 there were over 55,000 social enterprises, some of which also come into the categories of VCOs or cooperatives. The annual turnover of social enterprises is around £27 billion and they contribute about £8.4 billion to GDP. Social enterprises are active in a wide range of economic activity, in sectors such as training, social care, housing, leisure and childcare. They include organisations such as those selling fair trade goods such as Café Direct, organisations established to provide employment opportunities for people facing disadvantage (Social Firms) and development trusts.

Cooperatives and mutuals – as at December 2005 there were over 8,100 Industrial and Provident Societies registered with the Financial Services Authority, with around 19 million members. The most significant are consumer and worker cooperatives, cooperative consortiums, agricultural cooperatives and housing cooperatives. There were 567 registered credit unions in Great Britain as at September 2006, with just under ½ million members.

---

[3] Equalities groups refer to those groups who define themselves as representing marginalised communities, including women's groups, black and minority ethnic groups, lesbian, gay, bisexual and transgender communities, disability groups and refugee and asylum seeker groups.

[4] Sources of information: Charity Commission, NCVO, Annual Small Business Survey, Financial Services Authority

1.5 The first stage of consultation invited responses on the range of roles the third sector plays in society and across the spectrum of challenges faced by the sector. The consultation generated thousands of ideas and comments from the diversity of organisations in the third sector, some very specific to organisational type or interest but the majority reflecting common concerns and issues.

Interim report of the third sector review

1.6 The interim report of the third sector review brought together the most consistent messages from the consultation. This included setting out that the Government had heard the sectors' concerns over the sustainability of funding agreements, the importance of maintaining the principle of grant funding for smaller organisations, the inconsistency of relationships between the sector and different levels of Government, and a lack of mutual understanding between different parts of the sector and Government. Overall, however, the consultation also demonstrated the range of activities the third sector is involved in, the commitment of the workforce and the volunteers in the third sector and a strong desire for continued partnership working between the sector and Government, building on the significant progress that has been made.

1.7 A fuller summary of the responses to the third sector review consultation, building on the interim report, was published on the HM Treasury and Cabinet Office websites in June 2007.[5]

---

[5] Consultation feedback on the future role of the third sector in social and economic regeneration, HM Treasury, Cabinet Office, June 2007.

Box 1.2 The Last Ten Years – building the partnership between the third sector and Government

The Government has put in place a variety of measures to build a partnership with the third sector and to invest in promoting and growing the sector:

The **Charities Act**, which received Royal Assent in November 2006, reforms charity law to enable charities to administer themselves more efficiently, to improve the regulation of charity fundraising, and reduce regulation on the sector, especially for smaller charities, to provide a clear definition of charity with an emphasis on public benefit and to modernise the Charity Commission's functions and powers.

The 1998 **Compact** on relations between Government and the Voluntary Sector in England, jointly published with the sector and the Compact Codes, provide a framework to guide partnership working between the state and the third sector. Local Compacts, now operational or in development in 99 per cent of local authority areas, are local level agreements for partnership working. The **Commissioner for the Compact** is now taking forward the implementation of the Compact principles and will champion their dissemination and application across Government.

The **2002 and 2004 cross cutting reviews** of the role of the sector in public service delivery laid the foundations for an increased recognition of the role of the sector in the transformation of public services and investment in the capacity of the sector. **Futurebuilders** provides access to loan capital and **Capacitybuilders** invests in the sector's infrastructure. The **Action Plan for Third Sector Public Service Delivery** published in December 2006, sets out measures to further improve the commissioning and procurement landscape, bringing together activity from across Government. Since 1998, the **Invest to Save Budget** has allocated over £100 million to innovative service delivery initiatives involving third sector organisations.

The **2002 strategy for success** and subsequent 2006 **Social Enterprise Action Plan** set out a vision for a dynamic and sustainable social enterprise sector strengthening an inclusive and growing economy. The Action Plan sets out measures to promote the value of social enterprise, to improve the provision of information and advice to social enterprises, to enable access to finance and to promote further collaboration between social enterprise and Government. In 2005, the Government launched the **Community Interest Company**, providing a new lightly regulated legal form for social enterprise.

The **Getting Britain Giving** package announced in Budget 2000 made a number of changes to make the tax effective giving framework more generous and flexible and has been followed up by a series of technical changes and promotional work, including the **Giving Campaign** and the **Payroll Giving Grants Scheme** to encourage a greater culture of giving.

In recognition of the benefits of volunteering and mentoring, the Government has invested in increasing the number and quality of volunteering opportunities and increasing awareness and understanding of the benefits of voluntary activity to a diverse range of groups. This includes working with socially excluded groups through the **Volunteering For All** programme and in promoting and celebrating volunteering through the **2005 Year of the Volunteer.** Following the recommendations of the **Russell Commission** report on youth action and engagement, significant investment has been made in developing a framework for youth volunteering, building on the **Millennium Volunteers** programme and now being taken forward by youth volunteering organisation **v**.

1.8   The consultation has also fed into continuing policy development over the last year, including the Social Enterprise Action Plan, the Action Plan for Third Sector Public Service Delivery and key announcements made in the 2006 Pre-Budget Report and the 2007 Budget. Details of the measures in these publications are set out throughout this final report of the third sector review.

1.9   The interim report identified areas of work requiring further investigation and set out a series of questions the Government, working with the sector, wanted to examine. In the second phase of the review from December 2006, the Government has undertaken a programme of work drawing on a number of sources including:

- new research commissioned to support the review, including on the role of small community groups in the sector, the effectiveness of different funding mechanisms for the community sector and on voice and campaigning;

- further analysis of the consultation responses received, available research and evaluations;

- responses to the specific questions posed in the interim report, via the web-based questionnaire;

- meetings of the third sector advisory panel; and,

- focused thematic roundtable discussions, held around the country, led by members of the third sector advisory panel and involving key experts and stakeholders on each theme.

VISION FOR THE FUTURE ROLE OF THE THIRD SECTOR AND THE ROLE OF GOVERNMENT

A framework for partnership working

1.10   The third sector makes an enormous contribution to our society, economy and environment. Hundreds of thousands of organisations and millions of volunteers make a practical difference in communities, from working with young people to developing new ways of recycling household waste. The contribution of volunteers alone is estimated to be equivalent to over a million people working full time.[6] Third sector organisations also drive and energise many of the most important changes in our society, from campaigns such as Make Poverty History to encouraging people to quit smoking. Further, the sector makes an increasing contribution to our economy. For example, social enterprises now account for around 5 per cent of all businesses with employees, and have a turnover of over £27 billion a year.[7] As a consequence of these activities, the sector brings people together from different backgrounds, helping strengthen the social fabric of communities and the country.

1.11   Whilst welcoming and celebrating this contribution, it is not the Government's role to define the purposes of individual organisations or set a vision for the sector as a whole. That comes from the sector itself.

---

[6] The UK Voluntary Sector Almanac, NCVO, 2007.

[7] Annual Small Business Survey, Department of Trade and Industry, 2005.

1.12   However, the Government and the third sector work in partnership to improve society, sustain the environment and establish new forms of enterprise. The third sector review therefore sets out a framework for working in partnership with the sector over the next ten years, drawing on proposals made by thousands of people during the consultation process and a wider analysis of the opportunities and challenges facing the country.

The third sector today

1.13   Over the last decade, the third sector has grown significantly:

- the number of registered charities rose from around 120,000 in 1995 to over 160,000 in 2005. There are around 55,000 social enterprises.[8] In addition, there are hundreds of thousands of small community groups.

- the number of people volunteering formally or informally at least once a month rose from 18.4 million in 2001 to 20.4 million in 2005.[9] Charitable giving has kept up with the growth in GDP in recent years, at around £9 billion in 2005-06.[10]

- research into charities estimates that turnover has increased from around £16 billion in 1997 to over £27 billion in 2004-05 and the workforce has increased by around a fifth.[11]

- the 2003-04 State of the Sector Panel survey of over three thousand third sector organisations found that 56 per cent of respondents reported an increase in activity in the previous year and 67 per cent had expectations of growth in the next three years. This compares with only 6 per cent who reported a decline in activity and 6 per cent who expected contraction in the next three years.[12]

1.14   More importantly, the impact of the sector is also growing. For example, one study of the sector in Birmingham concluded that over the last three decades it had become more active, better connected and more politically influential.[13] The sector has continued to be a pioneer in many areas, from groundbreaking social enterprises, such as the Eden Project, to introducing successful new ways of reducing re-offending.

1.15   Not every organisation has grown. In particular, recent analysis of Charity Commission data by the National Council for Voluntary Organisations (NCVO) highlights the rapid growth of many large charities and the decline in the income of many small or medium-sized charities.[14] However, by most indicators England has one of the strongest sectors among developed countries.[15]

---

[8] Annual Small Business Survey, Department for Trade and Industry, 2005

[9] 2005 Citizenship Survey, DCLG, June 2006.

[10] UK Giving 2005/06, Charities Aid Foundation/NCVO, 2006.

[11] The UK Voluntary Sector Almanac, NCVO, 2007.

[12] News from the Panel (no.2) Activities and change in resources, Cabinet Office, August 2006.

[13] 'Social Capital and Urban Governance: Adding a more contextualized 'top down' perspective' Political Studies Volume **48** Maloney, W; Smith, G & Stoker, G 2000, cited in Improving small scale grant funding for local voluntary and community organisations, Discussion paper, Young Foundation, March 2007.

[14] The UK Voluntary Sector Almanac, NCVO, 2007.

[15] The Third Sector and Volunteering in Global Perspective, Presentation to the 17th Annual International Association of Volunteer Effort Conference, Amsterdam. Salamon, L. M. 2001.

Four common goals for the future

1.16 The third sector review has identified four major areas of common interest between the sector and Government: enabling greater voice and campaigning, strengthening communities, transforming public services, and encouraging social enterprise. These form the basis of the Government's proposed framework for partnership over the next ten years.

Enabling voice and campaigning **1.17** Most people desire to have a greater say over issues that affect their lives, but many feel that they are not currently able to do so.[16] For example, in one recent survey only a third of respondents considered that they could influence decisions affecting their area.[17] Participating in third sector organisations is an important way of achieving such influence at a local and national level and over the last decade, the role of the sector has been substantial, from fighting for equal rights to shaping local regeneration programmes.[18] The third sector review has identified a desire in much of the sector to further increase their campaigning and advocacy role. The recent report of the sector-led Advisory Group on Campaigning and the Voluntary Sector, chaired by Baroness Helena Kennedy, is just one example of that interest.

1.18 The Government welcomes this role for the sector. The Government seeks to support a vibrant democracy and civic society, enabling people to better participate in solving local and national issues and considers that the third sector plays a critical role in this process. The vision for partnership over the next ten years is to ensure that third sector organisations are able to play a growing role in civic society, better engage with decision makers and are never hindered from speaking out and representing their members, users and communities.

Strengthening communities **1.19** The third sector review has found much evidence of strong community life in England today, with rising levels of active citizenship and volunteering. However, there are also potential strains on the connections in society. Lifestyles and working patterns are increasingly varied. In some areas, the global rise in migration has led to far greater ethnic diversity than in previous decades. There is the risk that tensions develop between groups, as the independent Commission on Integration and Cohesion recently highlighted.[19] This is not simply a matter of ethnicity or race, in many areas, age or income are far more significant dividers.

1.20 Third sector organisations often help strengthen communities as well as delivering specific activities. For example, the environmental organisation Groundwork has found that among their tens of thousands of volunteers, over a third report making contact with people new to their neighbourhoods.[20] More generally, those who volunteer regularly are significantly more likely to trust others than those who do not.[21] The consultation conducted as part of the third sector review found that many in the sector share a broad objective of people from all backgrounds working together to make a difference in their communities. This is an objective that the Government shares. The

---

[16] Together We Can YouGov poll, March 2005.

[17] User Satisfaction and Local Government Service Provision, Communities and Local Government, 2006.

[18] Chanan found that volunteering and participating in third sector organisations was an important way of influencing local decisions, Measures of Community – A study for the Active Communities Directorate and the Research Development and Statistics Directorate of the Home Office, Gabriel Chanan, Community Development Foundation, 2004.

[19] Commission on Integration and Cohesion - Our shared future, Commission on Integration and Cohesion, June 2007.

[20] Third Sector Strategy for Communities and Local Government, Discussion Paper, Communities and Local Government, June 2007.

[21] 2005 Citizenship Survey, DCLG, June 2006.

vision for partnership over the next ten years is to enable third sector organisations to foster greater shared action between different sections of the community, and work with Local Government, public services and others to promote understanding and relationships across society.

Transforming public services
1.21 Some people consider that the third sector's direct contributions to society should be kept entirely separate from the State. However, the leaders of tens of thousands of third sector organisations have found that they can effectively meet their objectives and support their beneficiary groups by providing some services in partnership with the State. The third sector review consultation highlighted the continued desire of many third sector organisations to deliver their objectives by helping design or deliver better public services.

1.22 The Government considers that public service delivery by the sector can bring significant benefits if organisations wish to enter such partnerships. Such involvement is not about Government abdicating its responsibility to adequately fund public services. Instead, it is about ensuring that, in the right circumstances, the sector can deliver services where it is best placed to do so. In particular, recent research by the National Consumer Council found that some, although not all, third sector organisations develop better relationships with their users.[22]

1.23 Greater involvement in improving public services is not, however, confined to directly delivering services. As importantly, sector organisations can often be a catalyst for change as:

- partners in innovation;

- partners in designing services; and,

- campaigners for change.

1.24 The vision for partnership over the next ten years reflects all these roles; ensuring that public services are able to improve further by fully drawing on the understanding and experience of third sector in designing, developing and delivering services.

Encouraging social enterprise
1.25 Social enterprise has a long history, from the cooperative movement and mutual organisations of the nineteenth century to the long-standing trading activities of many charities. Over the last few years, one of the most important and exciting developments in the third sector has been an acceleration of interest and innovation in social enterprise. These include community enterprises such as development trusts, new providers of public services, such as GP cooperatives, and an expansion of consumer-focused enterprises, such as Café Direct. These organisations are creating new ways of delivering social and environmental outcomes through business approaches. They are both leading and responding to a rise in "ethical" markets, such as fair trade produce and ethical investments, which reached a total estimated value of nearly £30 billion in 2005, up 11 per cent on the previous year.[23] They are providing new outlets for employees who wish to combine social, environmental and business objectives.

---

22 Delivering Public Services, service users' experience of the third sector, National Consumer Council, 2007.

23 The Ethical Consumerism Report 2006, The Co-operative Bank, 2006.

1.26   The third sector review has highlighted the opportunities for further growth in social enterprise driven by developments such as the continued likely expansion of environmental and other ethical markets, the desire of commissioners to procure public services that meet wider social needs and new forms of social investment.

1.27   The Government has a role in working in partnership with the sector to help create the conditions to realise these opportunities. Entrepreneurs are not always aware of the potential and do not always consider social enterprise approaches. Access to appropriate finance and business support is also critical. The vision for partnership over the next ten years is of creating the conditions for the development of thousands more social enterprises and enabling those organisations that wish to diversify their income streams to undertake more trading activity.

Building the partnership   **1.28**   Box 1.2 highlights some of the measures the Government has introduced over the last ten years to support and work with the third sector. The growth in the size and impact of the sector over this time suggests that the approach in place has been successful. The third sector review therefore signals the Government's continuation of a number of important policies and programmes. These include, for example, continuing to strengthen the implementation of the Compact, further funding for the youth volunteering charity **v**, investment in capacity building, and the further support for organisations involved in the delivery of public services. However, this strategy also represents some important developments in the Government's approach. In addition to a series of specific measures, such as greater support for grant funding of small organisations, a new skills strategy and a new drive to improve research on the third sector, there are three cross cutting themes in how the Government wants to develop its partnership with the sector:

- working with a fuller range of organisations and supporting a wider range of activities by the sector, particularly community action and campaigning;

- a greater emphasis on investing in the long term sustainability of the third sector's work; and,

- a greater focus on local partnership working.

1.29   Key measures in the third sector review are summarised in Box 1.3.

Working with a fuller range of organisations and supporting a wider range of activities by the sector

1.30   The last two major Government cross-cutting reviews of the sector in 2002 and 2004 focused on enabling better public service delivery by the sector, reflecting the opportunities that have opened up in public service reform.[24] This work on public services has been complemented by specific strategies for social enterprise, youth volunteering and charitable giving.

---

[24] The role of the Voluntary and Community Sector in Service Delivery: a Cross Cutting Review, HM Treasury 2002 and Exploring the role of the Third Sector in Public Service Delivery and Reform, a Discussion Document, HM Treasury 2005.

1.31   The third sector review sets out measures to maintain progress on the opportunities highlighted in these previous cross cutting reviews, but also heralds a much wider interest in working with the sector. In particular, the Government is committed to expanding partnerships to build stronger communities and enable greater campaigning, alongside continued work on public service delivery, social enterprise and volunteering. The third sector review also highlights the Government's recognition of the contribution of a range of different types of third sector organisations: big and small, local and national, social enterprises, charities and community groups. The Government does not wish to favour one part of the sector over another.

A greater emphasis on investing in long term sustainability

1.32   In the past, too many partnerships and programmes have been short term. Future policies will put far greater emphasis on the sustainability of the third sector's work, including by shifting more resources to investing in the underlying strength of the sector and by ensuring that specific partnerships are for a sufficiently long period. For example, some of the most important measures in the third sector review are:

- building up the endowments of local foundations, to provide a long term income stream to small groups;

- promoting asset development, to give groups an independent basis for community action;

- enabling a growth in income generation by third sector organisations, particularly through social investment;

- investing in sector skills;

- investing in the evidence base; and,

- ensuring that three year funding relationships between Government and the third sector become the norm.

Local partnership working

1.33   Over the last few years, the Government has put particular effort into improving partnerships at a national level. For example, the Compact has been developed most effectively at national level, many Government Departments have developed important forums for considering policy, national programmes such as Capacitybuilders and Futurebuilders have been established and the regulatory environment has been strengthened.

1.34   Over the next ten years, the focus needs to be more on local partnerships. Some progress has already been made. For example, 99 per cent of Local Authorities now have a local Compact in place or in development. However, as central Government devolves more decision making to the local level, it is important that new measures focus on the local. That is why the recent Local Government White Paper set out new duties on Local Authorities to inform, consult and involve local citizens. The third sector review builds on that work. Over the next few years, the Government will seek to ensure greater incentives for good local partnerships. The development of new programmes, such as the small grants and endowments programmes, are also focused on developing capacity at local level. Finally, the Government will focus capacity building work with the third sector and public agencies at the front line.

Box 1.3 Summary of key measures in the third sector review

The final report of the third sector review sets out a series of measures to build the partnership with the third sector. The key announcements are:

- a new focus on enabling the third sector's role in campaigning and voice activity, including investment in innovative consultation approaches and better using the Compact to protect the right of organisations to campaign;

- a new £50m local endowment match fund enabling local independent foundations to develop community endowments to provide sustainability in future grant making, building on the £80 million small grants programme for community action and voice announced in Budget 2007;

- at least £10 million of new investment in community anchor organisations and community asset and enterprise development, building on the £30 million Community Assets Fund announced in the 2006 Pre-Budget Report;

- £117m of new resources for youth volunteering, building on the work of **v**, alongside other volunteering programmes;

- building capacity of third sector organisations to improve public services, through the Futurebuilders Fund, training for public sector Commissioners and work to build the evidence on opportunities for the third sector;

- additional investment to raise awareness of the social enterprise business model and support for Government Departments to investigate areas for social enterprise delivery;

- better mechanisms to drive best practice in funding the third sector, including in the expectation that when Government Departments and their agencies receive their 2008-11 budgets, they will pass on that three year funding to third sector organisations that they fund, as the norm;

- a new programme to build the third sector evidence base, including a new national research centre;

- a new third sector skills strategy;

- over £85 million of new investment for third sector infrastructure development through Capacitybuilders, with new programmes on voice and campaigning, social enterprise and a focus on reaching down to the smallest community groups; and,

- continued focus on the Compact as a means to build the relationship between the third sector and all levels of Government.

PURPOSE OF THIS REPORT

1.35   This report concludes the work of the third sector review. It sets out the results of the second stage of analysis and consultation under the five themes of the review, building on the messages set out in the interim report. The report sets out the areas where Government will build on its investments in the third sector to date through the Office of the Third Sector in Cabinet Office and new priority areas for the 2007 CSR years that have been identified by the review. The report also sets out action across a range of Government Departments and their agencies working with the third sector.

1.36   Chapters 2-6 set out the actions and priorities for Government within the main themes of the review. Chapter 7 summarises the key actions for the Office of the Third Sector and sets out some important milestones.

1.37   Implementation of the third sector review will be a collaborative process and feedback is welcome at:

- http://haveyoursay.cabinetoffice.gov.uk/third_sector/

2

ENABLING VOICE AND CAMPAIGNING

Summary

The Government recognises the role of the third sector organisations in representing the voices of different groups and in campaigning to achieve change for individuals and communities.

The Government will:

- revise methods of consultation and invest in research to better understand the most effective methods of consulting with a range of organisations;

- undertake work to understand how Government and the sector are ensuring the right of organisations to campaign for change, through implementation of the Compact principles;

- through Capacitybuilders invest in capacity building support for organisations undertaking campaigning work;

- provide support for organisations wishing to promote innovative approaches to campaigning activity;

- work with the Charity Commission to update guidance on political activities and campaigning by charities, taking into account the recommendations of the Advisory Group on Campaigning and the Voluntary Sector;

- provide and promote strategic funding for partner organisations to enable them to input into policy making; and,

- create a new advisory structure for Ministers to hear from third sector organisations on policy issues.

INTRODUCTION

2.1   The role of the third sector in providing a means for individuals and communities to make their voices heard and in promoting those voices to campaign for change is critical in supporting civil renewal. The Government wants to promote the development of strong, active and empowered communities, where people are able to define the problems they face and in partnership with public bodies, enable positive change. Organisations that represent the voices of their community and campaign for change are a vital part of the democratic process, articulating concerns in a way that holds statutory agencies to account and feed into and improve the policy making process. This role is particularly important in respect of groups that currently may feel marginalised in decision making, due to disadvantage or discrimination.

2.2   The Campaigning Effectiveness programme at the National Council for Voluntary Organisations (NCVO) views campaigning as; a range of activities by organisations 'to influence others in order to effect an identified and desired social, economic, environmental or political change'.[1] Many organisations in the third sector are equipped to influence public policy and drive social change through campaigning activity, whether it be through research, policy development, lobbying, membership

---

[1] The Good Campaigns Guide, NCVO, 2005.

and public action, media work and communications. Through these mechanisms, organisations provide voice to communities and individuals' interests sometimes in response to and within governments' public policy making agenda and sometimes outside of these boundaries. There are also significant examples of the Government and third sector organisations joining together to campaign for change.

2.3   However, there are many organisations that do not feel as if the voices of their members, communities or users are heard adequately and who do not have the resources available to them to campaign for change. The Government recognises that there are multiple voices and a diversity of interests within the third sector and that additional resources may be required to reach and understand the range of views on an issue.

THE CONSULTATION

2.4   The key messages from the consultation on issues of voice and campaigning, as highlighted in the interim report of the third sector review are:

- although the level of consultation by Government has been increasing significantly over recent years, more needs to be done to ensure that there is clarity as to the action that is taken as a result of the consultation. The Government often seeks the views of third sector organisations but must do more to recognise the multiplicity of views and to demonstrate active listening and responding to those views;

- the third sector is often critical in enabling and empowering individuals and communities to make their voices heard through campaigning and active participation. However to promote this further, particularly amongst groups that feel that their voices are weaker, there is a need for appropriate learning opportunities and capacity building. Organisations also report difficulties in accessing appropriate funding for campaigning type activities and may sometimes feel constrained in the voice and campaigning role by certain funding or contracting arrangements;

- there is a lack of clarity around the legislative and regulatory framework for campaigning; and,

- there is a desire among third sector organisations that where they have similar objectives or opinions, they should seek to join their voices together to more effectively work with Government and campaign for change.

2.5   The thematic roundtable discussion on voice and campaigning[2] underlined the need for increased mutual understanding between the sector and Government and that Government needs to listen to the diversity of voices in communities. Calls were made for fewer but better and deeper consultations on issues and for capacity building support and skills development for the third sector in voice and campaigning. Many people who want to campaign at a local level, have little idea about how to go about it or who to turn to. The roundtable also highlighted a challenge to the third sector to ensure they are representing fully the views and voices of those that they purport to.

---

[2] Held in Newcastle in March 2007 and chaired by Stuart Etherington of the National Council for Voluntary Organisations.

THE FUTURE ROLE OF THE THIRD SECTOR IN VOICE AND CAMPAIGNING

2.6   Over the next ten years, the Government wants to see greater recognition of the multiple voices present in and represented by the third sector, alongside building a culture where the Government understands and celebrates the right of third sector organisations to campaign for change. The Government recognises that the closeness of many third sector organisations to their beneficiaries, whether through service provision, community ownership or advocacy often puts organisations in a unique position to inform and influence policy making and to campaign for change.

2.7   The Government wants to work towards enhanced consultation processes with the third sector so that more voices can be heard, in conjunction with greater transparency around the action that Government takes as a result of consultation. The Government also wants to create the right enabling environment for organisations to provide voice to citizens and to campaign, including through capacity building and increased opportunities for learning and by continuing to ensure that organisations are able to operate within an appropriate and proportionate legislative and regulatory environment. The Government is also determined to ensure that the Compact principles explicitly setting out the sector's right to campaign and comment on Government policy are enforced throughout Government.

Communication and consultation – a listening and responsive Government

2.8   The Government recognises that listening and responding to the views of citizens and communities is a vital part of the policy making process and a thriving democracy. Work undertaken by the Campaigning Effectiveness programme at NCVO and the Sheila McKechnie Foundation suggests that at their best consultations can provide the opportunity for third sector organisations to have their views formally recorded, listened to, and taken into account and to have their recommended policy prescriptions considered and incorporated within public policy making.[3] Consultations can also help identify the balance of popular opinion on certain issues.

Diverse voices   **2.9**   There remains however, a need to continue to drive best practice in consulting and in feeding back to participants. It is also important that Government continues to recognise and hear multiple voices, including from marginalised groups and from the smallest organisations. Some current consultation process may act to detract from the third sector's capacity to represent the voices of different groups, only involving a small number of organisations with the resources to input. In order for the voices of more disadvantaged communities to be heard, Government and to some extent larger and representative organisations within the third sector need to think creatively and take active steps to reach communities.

2.10   *Strong and Prosperous Communities*, the Local Government White Paper, sets out explicitly the Government's commitment to empower communities to have greater influence over decisions that affect them.[4] It proposes a new duty on Local Government to consult and involve local people in their policy development, new instruments such as the Community Call for Action, access to a general power of wellbeing for quality parish/neighbourhood councils and encourages the development of local charters.

---

[3] Understanding the role of Government in relation to voice and campaigning, Campaigning Effectiveness, NCVO and Sheila McKechnie Foundation, February 2007.

[4] Strong and prosperous communities. The Local Government White Paper, Communities and Local Government, 2006.

Best practice in consultation

2.11   The Code of Practice on Consultation was first published in November 2000 outlining minimum standards for central Government Departments and their agencies when they are carrying out national, written consultation exercises. A revised Code was published in January 2004 and Government Departments are required to provide information regarding their adherence to the Code in their annual reports. The Cabinet Office is now undertaking a new consultation exercise to invite views on reviewing the Code of Practice on Consultation.[5] The consultation recognises that current practices can be improved upon, with feedback from stakeholders suggesting that a 12 week written consultation is sometimes on its own not enough, may sometimes be superfluous to requirements and is not always the more effective way of getting views from those who might be affected by what is being discussed. The consultation seeks views on issues such as consultation fatigue, how to raise awareness of consultation exercises and ways, other than written consultation of seeking input from those voices who would otherwise go unheard. The consultation puts forward three options for consideration for a revised Code. These options are:

- requiring Government Departments to undertake written consultation plus one other method;

- a Code of Practice with a fast-track consultation procedure specified for certain consultations; and

- a principles based approach, where the criteria in the current Code are replaced with a set of core principles that would have to be taken into account by Government Departments when consulting.

2.12   Building on this work to drive better consultation practices across Government, the Government recognises that all Government Departments and their agencies need to take active steps to involve the views of a range of diverse voices within the third sector as an integral part of the policy making process. This will require innovative consultation methods to ensure that policy making reaches out to some of the smaller and more marginalised groups in the sector, including faith and equalities groups. Communities and Local Government (CLG) are taking work forward in this area through their on-line discussion forum, which is being used as one of the ways the Department is seeking feedback on their third sector strategy.[6]

2.13   To support this, the Office of the Third Sector will:

- invest in research to promote better understanding of innovative and effective methods of consultation and engagement with the third sector, and;

- will act as an exemplar of best practice in consulting and feeding back to the sector, building on the consultation undertaken as part of the third sector review. In the first instance the Office of the Third Sector will, test different methods of consultation with the sector on the new programme to raise awareness of social enterprise. Further details of this programme are set out in Chapter 5.

---

[5] Effective consultation, asking the right questions, asking the right people, listening to the answers. Cabinet Office, June 2007.

[6] Available at www.communities.gov.uk

Box 2.1 Faith and equalities based groups

The consultation for the third sector review highlighted there are some groups in the third sector who feel that they are disadvantaged, particularly in relation to accessing mainstream grant funding. These included many faith-based organisations and groups representing marginalised communities, such as black and minority ethnic groups, women's organisations, disability groups and lesbian, gay, bisexual and transgender communities.

The Government will seek to ensure continued dialogue with these groups and that all of the measures announced in the third sector review will be as accessible as possible to a wide range of organisations.

Communities and Local Government (CLG) has overarching responsibility for engaging with faith communities. The specific aims of CLG's engagement with faith communities are to:

- increase faith communities' contribution to active citizenship and community cohesion; role as agents of change within communities; and provision of services as part of the Voluntary and Community Sector;

- draw in the other faiths to work alongside, and support, Muslim communities in addressing radicalisation and extremism;

- develop a role for faith communities in wider social action and regeneration; and

- ensure there is effective consultation and co-operation between Government Departments and faith communities and to promote best practice in this.

CLG is currently working on an interfaith strategy, due to be completed in the autumn of 2007, which will clearly define Government policy on its aims and objectives in supporting interfaith and intercultural dialogue.

CLG works closely with faith leaders and representatives of main faith communities to ensure that national policies reflect the needs of local communities. The Faith Communities Consultative Council (FCCC) for example acts as a streamlined national structure for Government to engage with faith communities, monitor consultation and receive feedback from national faith representatives. The FCCC includes representatives from the nine main world faiths.

Enabling and empowering citizens and communities

2.14   The success and profile of numerous third sector led campaigns demonstrates the effectiveness with which some organisations in the sector can mobilise resources and use their expertise to influence public policy making and wider society. However, it is also clear that many organisations lack the capacity and the skills to undertake campaigning activity. The Campaigning Effectiveness/Sheila McKechnie Foundation study identifies several key areas where the capacity of organisations could be enhanced, alongside some specific barriers to the sector's voice and campaigning roles.

Barriers to active voice and campaigning   2.15   For some organisations, basic knowledge of campaigning needs to be improved, with organisations finding it difficult to recognise who to influence and the best means of going about it. There is evidence to suggest that community-based campaigns find it particularly difficult to project their voices to decision makers and lack access to appropriate capacity building opportunities. A survey undertaken by People and Planet and the Sheila McKechnie Foundation found that 35 per cent of organisations with turnover of less than £500,000 said that they did not have the skills to campaign.[7]

2.16   Other organisations have cited difficulties in campaigning, which can be grouped under:

- funding campaigns (the survey cited above found that 47 per cent of organisations agreed with the statement "we don't have the funds to campaign");

- the nature of funding or contracting agreements, which can sometimes be perceived as limiting the sector's independence in its campaigning role;

- capacity building – particularly the need for investment in innovation and learning;

- overcoming real or perceived legal barriers to campaigning; and

- internal organisational or sector based challenges such as the challenges of working in partnership with others to deliver campaigns, and issues around campaign selection, securing internal buy-in and the appropriate processes for campaigns.

2.17   The Government's role over the long-term is to support an enabling environment in which third sector organisations can actively play the voice and campaigning role that they wish to. The Government can in this regard take action in capacity building and breaking down some of the barriers that prevent the third sector taking this active role.

Funding relationships   **2.18**   The new £80 million fund announced at Budget 2007 to provide small grants to promote community action and voice will over the 2007 CSR years provide a platform for small organisations to contribute to building strong and active communities, in part through providing voice for underrepresented groups and undertaking local campaigns to achieve change in communities. The funding will be channelled through local independent grant funders, such as Community Foundations. Further details of the fund are set out in Chapter 3.

2.19   The Government also wants to take steps to build a culture that recognises the value of voice and campaigning activity by the third sector. It will seek, in its dealings with the sector, to act in ways that protect and increase the sector's ability both to play an independent role in communities and to contribute to the delivery of services. These aims, and related provisions in the Compact and its Codes, continue to apply whether or not there is a formal funding or contracting relationship with an organisation. The proposed review of the Compact and its Codes (see Chapter 6) must ensure that these principles, including the independence of the third sector and its right to undertake campaigns, regardless of any funding relationship with Government, are preserved and reaffirmed.

2.20   All Government Departments and their agencies should recognise the independence of the third sector and the right for third sector organisations to campaign. They should handle all their dealings with the sector in a manner, which reflects their wider responsibility to protect and increase the sector's ability both to

---

[7] Barriers to Campaigning: Survey of Voluntary Organisations Attitudes to Campaigning and the Law, People and Planet, Sheila McKechnie Foundation, 2006.

play an independent role in communities and to contribute to the delivery of services. The Commissioner for the Compact has a role in monitoring progress in this area.

2.21 To build understanding of how Government and third sector organisations are adhering to the principles of the Compact governing voice and campaigning, the Office of the Third Sector with key partners such as Communities and Local Government, and consulting the Commissioner for the Compact, will undertake a programme of learning and development around how the Compact is being implemented. This will inform further work over the 2007 CSR years around promoting the role of the third sector in enabling voice and campaigning.

Box 2.2 The third sector voice in tackling climate change

The third sector has a critical role in engaging, enabling and encouraging wider action on climate change and the environment. Third sector organisations connect and engage with hundreds of thousands of people, supporting them as individuals, and mobilising them as a growing environmental movement. Around two fifths of national greenhouse gas emissions result directly from decisions taken by individuals, whom third sector organisations can inform and encourage to make low carbon choices - particularly around travel and energy in the home. As trusted organisations with established and growing audiences, third sector organisations are particularly powerful communicators, giving a strong voice to all those concerned about climate change, and campaigning for solutions.

The third sector can also lead by example by adopting good practice on energy and the environment within their own operations. Many have already pledged to do so by signing up to the Third Sector Declaration on Climate Change launched in June 2007.

The Department for Environment, Food and Rural Affairs (Defra) has already been supporting third sector action on climate change and the environment through the Environmental Action Fund, Climate Challenge Fund and Every Action Counts initiative. Defra will be working with stakeholders to further explore the ways in which Defra and the third sector can work better together to mobilise action at the grassroots which helps people make more informed day to day decisions to tackle climate change.

2.22 Parts of the third sector lack access to appropriate learning and capacity building opportunities to allow them to develop the skills for campaigning. As set out in the interim report of the third sector review the Government is taking action to enhance the citizenship skills of adults through the new national framework – Take Part,[8] and through improvements to citizenship education in schools, following on from the independent diversity and citizenship review, led by Keith Ajegbo. Citizenship is proving to be a successful and popular course subject and with the Qualification and Curriculum Authority (QCA) the Department for Children, Schools and Families (DCSF) is developing a full course GCSE and an A level. The QCA is also working up a module for active citizenship, primarily aimed at post-16 learners, in line with wider reforms of 14-19 and post-19 qualifications.

---

[8] www.takepart.org

2.23   Chapter 6 sets out details of work to be taken forward to develop a strategy for skills development in the third sector overall, being led by the Department for Innovation, Universities and Skills, in partnership with the Office of the Third Sector.

2.24   To support skills building at the individual level, Capacitybuilders will also through the 2007 CSR years, invest in infrastructure through its voice, campaigning and leadership programme to provide support to frontline organisations to undertake voice and campaigning work.

2.25   Third sector organisations also have opportunities to campaign in new ways, particularly through the increased use of electronic media such as the internet and mobile phone technology as a mechanism for bringing about the development of new internet forums and forms of campaigning such as e-petitions. Some organisations however are less familiar with the opportunities and challenges of this technology Supplementing capacity building work, the Office of the Third Sector will also provide support for organisations wishing to promote innovative approaches to third sector campaigning activity, over the 2007 CSR years.

Box 2.3 Promoting giving and volunteering in the citizenship curriculum – Giving Nation

Inspired by the Giving Campaign, funded by the Office of the Third Sector and the Department for Children, Schools and Families, and run by third sector organisation the Citizenship Foundation, Giving Nation celebrates the power of young people to shape their world through the voluntary giving of time, money and voice to help others.

This schools-based programme supports the teaching of the citizenship curriculum, providing free resources that promote charitable activity and community involvement, through decision-making, action and reflection.

Giving Nation is also developing an active learning programme that teaches about the third sector through the citizenship and enterprise curricula: the Giving Nation Challenge. This will bring together the goals of educating 11-19s about charities in the classroom and enlivening the school environment through extra curricular charitable activity. The first full year of use will be from September 2007. Schools using the challenge will automatically be entered in to the annual Giving Nation Awards.

The Citizenship Foundation has also developed curriculum materials for primary schools through 'Go-Givers'. Go Givers is delivered to classrooms through a dedicated website containing lesson plans for teachers and interactive involvement for children and parents.

www.g-nation.co.uk

www.gogivers.org

2.26 It is important that, in serving their charitable purpose, charities should be free to participate in appropriate ways in political activities. There are clear benefits to society from allowing and encouraging charities to do so. As the Charity Commission sets out: "….political campaigning is an entirely legitimate activity for a charity. It is often a highly effective means of pursuing a charitable purpose, even where the matters at issue are highly controversial. Charities have a vital role to play in society in promoting the interests of their beneficiaries and in contributing to public debate based on their experience of their beneficiaries' needs."[9]

2.27 The Charity Commission has, in 2004 and in early 2007, published new material designed to illustrate the considerable latitude that charities have for political campaigning under the existing rules, and to encourage charities to make use of that latitude. However, concerns remain within the sector that there is a wider range of legal and regulatory factors, including but not limited to the rules applying to charities, that unjustifiably restricts political campaigning by third sector organisations. An Advisory Group on Campaigning and the Voluntary Sector, chaired by Baroness Kennedy QC, published its report on 23 May. The Advisory Group recommended, in summary:

- that "charities should be able to engage in political campaigning in furtherance of their charitable purposes as long as they do not support political parties";

- changes to a number of statutory provisions, and to policing procedures and codes of practice, to liberalise the regime for controlling protests and demonstrations; and,

- changes to the Communications Act 2003 to liberalise the regime for controlling "political" advertising by non-governmental organisations and charities on radio and television.

Political activity **2.28** The rules on political campaigning by charities derive from case law and are not easy for charities to find or to understand without interpretation and explanation. Most charities rely on the Charity Commission's guidance *Campaigning and Political Activities by Charities (CC9)* and the questions and answers accompanying the guidance. The Commission's guidance sets out the basic principles that:

- to be a charity an organisation must have exclusively charitable purposes;

- the law does not regard any political purpose as being a charitable purpose;

- therefore an organisation which has a political purpose cannot be a charity;

- a charity may not support or oppose any political party; but

- a charity is allowed to use political activities as means of achieving its charitable purposes.

2.29 The important distinction here is between ends (or purposes) and means (or activities). A charity must not have, or pursue, political ends; but it may use some political means to achieve its charitable ends.

---

[9] Charity Commission: "Campaigning and political activities by charities: some questions and answers" (April 2007).

2.30   The Commission's guidance explains that political campaigning by a charity is acceptable provided that it is not "the dominant means by which a charity carries out its charitable purpose". Its basis for saying this is that, in a case where a charity is being run with political campaigning as its sole or predominant activity, those running the charity might be regarded as having in practice allowed charitable purposes to be supplanted by political purposes as the charity's reason for existing. That would not be acceptable, since a charity must not have a political purpose. However, it is surely possible, in a well-run charity, for political activity to be "dominant" within a charity and yet still enable it to further its charitable purpose.

2.31   The Government continues to believe that the law should not allow an organisation with a political purpose to be a charity. The fact that charities are not politically-motivated or -aligned is part of the reason why they enjoy a high level of public trust. The Government also believes that charities should be, and should feel, free to carry on political activities where those are effective means of pursuing their charitable purposes. Provided that the ultimate purpose remains demonstrably a charitable one the Government can see no objection, legal or other, to a charity pursuing that purpose wholly or mainly through political activities. Those running any charity have to justify its activities. If they can show that political activity, in preference to (or in conjunction with) any other type of activity, is likely to be effective in serving the charitable purpose then they will have succeeded in justifying the political activity. As the Charity Commission says, a charity which loses sight of its charitable purpose and allows political activity to take over as the end in itself has gone outside the bounds of what is acceptable for a charity. Whether or not that has happened in any individual case is for the Commission, as regulator, to decide.

2.32   **The Charity Commission is reviewing its guidance on political activities and campaigning by charities, and will publish this guidance in the autumn. The Commission has agreed, in reviewing its guidance, to consider the recommendations of the Advisory Group on Campaigning and the Voluntary Sector's report and to see if more can be done in the light of that report to clarify its guidance on charities and political campaigning.**

Restrictions on protests   **2.33**   The ability of citizens to campaign and protest is essential to a democracy. The Government has also therefore committed to consult widely on the provisions in the Serious Organised Crime and Police Act with a view to ensuring that people's right to protest is not subject to unnecessary restrictions. This review will need to reflect the security situation and allow the business of Parliament to proceed unhindered, but will be conducted with a presumption in favour of freedom of expression.[10]

Strategic third sector voices

2.34   The Office of the Third Sector funds a number of key strategic partners at national and regional level to ensure that the views of the sector can make an impact on the development of Government policy toward the sector. As set out in the interim report of the third sector review, this funding is for a minimum of three years and enables the Government to develop a more proactive joint approach to the needs and values of the sector. In 2007-08, this programme has allocated over £14 million to third sector organisations. The Government will continue the strategic partners programme into the 2007 CSR years.

---

[10] The Governance of Britain, HM Government, July 2007.

2.35 The Office of the Third Sector will champion and provide support to Government Departments wishing to provide strategic, long-term funding to third sector organisations to provide a consistent voice in public policy making, alongside the development or updating of Departmental third sector strategies.

2.36 As a first step, CLG has recognised, through their third sector strategy published in June 2007, the need for long-term strategic engagement with the third sector to bring greater coherence to policy development.[11] **CLG will develop a strategic partners programme for engaging third sector organisations, which provide a strategic voice and can support local action in the Department's policy areas.** Subject to the outcome of the 2007 CSR, CLG will develop a new Strategic Partners Grant Programme providing core funding over a three-year period for Strategic Partners and will encourage the pooling of small grants programmes to the third sector to provide greater certainty, efficiency and the potential to develop deeper relationships with the third sector. CLG will also establish a Third Sector Partnership Board of between 15-20 members to provide oversight and facilitate critical challenge between the third sector, Local Government and the Department.

---

[11] Third Sector Strategy for Communities and Local Government, Discussion paper, CLG, June 2007.

> **Box 2.4 Third sector voice in policy making – the Department for Environment, Food and Rural Affairs (Defra) and the Department for Work and Pensions (DWP)**
>
> Defra has a wide range of third sector stakeholders from small rural volunteer-led community groups to international environmental organisations. Defra seeks policy input from the third sector in a variety of ways:
>
> - a Compact Group, with representatives from the Department and the sector taking a proactive role in supporting Defra to mainstream the Compact principles, including through work to ensure third sector organisations can recover appropriate management and overhead costs in their funding agreements;
>
> - the Rural Community Buildings Network, comprised of representatives from faith groups and other third sector organisations whose assets include community buildings. The network brings together partners to share information and best practice on matters affecting rural community buildings and to provide a unified voice to advise on policy; and,
>
> - a Social Enterprise Stakeholders Forum to discuss taking forward the Departments' social enterprise agenda, as set out in the strategy *Social Enterprise – Securing the Future*, published in spring 2005.
>
> The Office for Disability Issues is also taking important steps to ensure that the voices of disabled people and their organisations are heard. The Prime Minister's Strategy Unit 2005 report *Improving the Life Chances of Disabled People* sets out the Government's vision for disabled people, that 'by 2025, disabled people in Britain should have full opportunities and choices to improve their quality of life and will be respected and included as equal members of society'. The report includes sixty recommendations for delivering their vision and for improving disabled people's lives, including the establishment of a "national forum for organisations of disabled people" to create an effective channel of communication between disabled people and Government.
>
> Equality 2025 - the UK Advisory Network on Disability Equality, was launched in December 2006, and currently comprises 22 disabled members. This advisory non-departmental public body will help Government understand the needs and wishes of disabled people, to enable the views of disabled people across the UK to inform and influence policy making and contribute to the development of policies and services.

2.37 A number of bodies currently exist to advise Ministers about aspects of their third sector policy:

- the Voluntary and Community Sector Advisory Group, which advises on voluntary and community sector policy and practice;

- the Futurebuilders Advisory Panel, which advises Ministers on the progress of the Futurebuilders programme and acts as a "critical friend" to the programme;

- the Infrastructure National Partnership which advises not only Ministers but also other Government bodies and Capacitybuilders on the strategy and implementation of the Government's ChangeUp capacity building programme, which is run by Capacitybuilders; and,

- the third sector review advisory group, which has advised Ministers on this review.

2.38 The Office of the Third Sector also benefits from the advice of its strategic partners – the third sector organisations that it funds to provide Government with the representative voice of their particular constituency within the sector, as set out above.

2.39 For the 2007 CSR years, the Office of the Third Sector will look to create a single advisory body, drawing in expertise from across the third sector. The new streamlined advisory structure will be established for the beginning of the 2007 CSR years.

3

STRENGTHENING COMMUNITIES

Summary

The Government recognises the role of community organisations in bringing people together and providing essential local services.

The Government will:

- take forward the £30 million Community Assets Fund to provide communities with the resources to develop community owned buildings, accessible to the whole community;

- work to build relationships between Local Authorities and local organisations, particularly through the new single performance framework for Local Authorities and work with the Audit Commission to develop proposals for Comprehensive Area Assessments that judge the effectiveness of local partnership working, including the involvement of the third sector;

- take forward the Budget 2007 announcement of an £80 million fund in small grants to community groups, through local grant funders to enable people and groups to make a difference in their local areas;

- invest £50 million in endowments for local independent foundations to ensure that they can provide grant funding for community groups into the future;

- provide resources to help community anchor organisations become sustainable through support to develop assets or generate income;

- work with funders to ensure they make full use of the flexibility offered in clawback rules;

- invest £117 million in the national framework for youth volunteering, run by the organisation **v**, providing thousands of opportunities for young people to get involved in their communities;

- work with the Volunteering Champion, Baroness Neuberger to promote volunteering in the public sector and to ensure Government Departments have plans in place to engage volunteers in the work of Departments;

- take forward an integrated programme to promote and support best practice in volunteering and mentoring, including the promotion of intergenerational volunteering; and,

- work with Capacitybuilders to ensure capacity building support is focused on delivering benefit to the frontline and reaches out to a diverse range of communities, including through investment in a modernised volunteering and third sector infrastructure.

INTRODUCTION

3.1   The Government wants to ensure that all communities can thrive, with the capacity to bring people together to deal with common concerns and achieve change. At the heart of this active participation of communities in civil renewal and neighbourhood regeneration are community based organisations providing the platform not only to meet the needs of individuals but for empowerment of individuals to bring about transformation of communities. Community organisations also act as a bridge between individuals and the state, providing opportunities for people to express their voices, building democratic engagement. The community sector – the range of organisations from volunteer led groups with little or no budget to large multipurpose community anchor organisations – is in this way rooted in the communities they serve, owned and led by community interests and is a key partner of Government, and particularly Local Government, in building strong, active and connected communities.

THE CONSULTATION

3.2   As set out in the interim report of the third sector review, the consultation highlighted:

- the value of maintaining a mix of simple and accessible grant funding, alongside the increased opportunities for contracting to deliver public services;

- the need for continued and enhanced representation of community based organisations representing different groups and interests in local decision making arenas, such as Local Strategic Partnerships and in the development of Local Area Agreements; and,

- that organisations representing marginalised groups feel that they encounter increased barriers to accessing mainstream Government grant funding;

- that grant funding for community organisations should sit alongside enhanced community capacity building, providing the practical support needed for people and organisations to tackle local problems;

- the importance of developing community assets to enable community organisations to generate their own wealth, become more enterprising, deliver services and strengthen community engagement and cohesion;

- the continuing need to break down the real and perceived barriers to active participation and volunteering in communities and to promote the benefits of voluntary action, particularly for those who may face additional difficulties to accessing opportunities;

3.3   The interim report of the third sector review set out initial measures to support community building, including an additional £6.5 million in 2007-08 within the Safer and Stronger Communities (SSC) block of Local Area Agreements.

Box 3.1 Funding through the Safer and Stronger Communities Fund

Following the announcement in the interim report of the third sector review, one project being funded through the Safer and Stronger Communities Fund is happening in the Bank End area of Barnsley. Voluntary Action Barnsley (the local Council for Voluntary Service) has joined forces with Barnsley Metropolitan Borough Council's community planning team to bring a neighbourhood management approach to the area.

£65,000 has been made available through the neighbourhood element of the Safer and Stronger Communities Fund and has been allocated to carry out intense community engagement; provide activities which will generate positive community spirit, work with residents and support them to lead and influence issues that affect their quality of life. Links with other local governance structures, such as the Area Board, will also be strengthened. In this way Barnsley Council is promoting community engagement and service delivery at a local level, by bringing together the third sector, service providers and the relatively small amount of funding needed for the project.

www.vabarnsley.org.uk

Community assets

3.4 Building on the measures set out in the Local Government White Paper, the principles of Firm Foundations,1 and now the recommendations of the Quirk Review on community management and ownership of assets, the interim report also announced the creation of a £30 million Community Assets Fund. The Quirk Review highlights the important role that assets can play in building communities through the generation of surpluses for the community, along with their role in bringing stability and sustainability to a community organisation and in facilitating partnership between local statutory agencies and the community.2 The Community Assets Fund will be delivered by the Big Lottery Fund, working in partnership with other organisations such as the Adventure Capital Fund to:

- improve the physical infrastructure available to local communities;

- empower community led third sector organisations to be innovative in responding to local needs, and enhance their capacity to tackle social disadvantage, transform lives and draw communities together;

- enable third sector organisations to strengthen their place in local communities – not only through increased capacity but also through greater independence and the opportunity to run a financially sustainable asset; and,

- benefit the wider community by raising the potential for job creation and further investment, and creating a focal point for local pride, confidence and cohesion.

---

1 Firm Foundations, published in 2004, is the Government's framework for community capacity building. It sets out a community development approach to strengthening the community sector with four key areas for action: appropriate and accessible learning opportunities for citizens and professional to equip them for community engagement; the development of community anchor organisations; the promotion of local action planning; and building links between community capacity building activity at a local, regional and national level.

2 Making assets work. The Quirk Review of community management and ownership of public assets, May 2007.

3.5 In March 2007, the Government published a consultation document seeking views on some aspects of how the Community Assets Fund will work, such as its beneficiaries, distribution and eligibility.[3] The consultation closed on 23rd June 2007 and the Office of the Third Sector will publish a summary of responses in the summer.

THE FUTURE ROLE OF THE THIRD SECTOR IN STRENGTHENING COMMUNITIES

3.6 Over the next ten years, the Government wants to put the third sector at the heart of work to build strong, active and connected communities, with Local Government as the most important driver in building this relationship. This is increasingly important over the coming years as communities face increased transition and socio-economic and demographic change, prompted by trends such as positive net inward migration of around 145,000 each year from 2008 and increased ethnic diversity. Many communities are already well placed to adapt to these changes with key factors contributing to community cohesion demonstrating progress, such as declining levels of crime and the fear of crime, fewer numbers of people reporting that they are racially prejudiced and levels active citizenship and volunteering increasing.[4]

3.7 Further consultation with the third sector and analysis has demonstrated that the range of organisations in the community sector play a vital role in strengthening communities, bringing people together from different backgrounds and empowering people to achieve change in communities. The Government believes that the contribution that local third sector organisations make in these areas provide the key rationale for direct provision of support to communities. Published alongside this final report of the third sector review a Young Foundation study commissioned for the review highlights where there is evidence on the outcomes and impacts of small community organisations in particular.[5]

Third sector building social capital

3.8 The study suggests that participation in community organisations can help to build trust and reciprocity in communities with evidence from the 2005 Citizenship Survey highlighting a positive relationship between having a sense of belonging to a neighbourhood and volunteering in the community along with an increased level of trust in other local people. Community organisations can also help to build individuals' confidence, particularly amongst those less likely to participate and can enable and boost civic participation whether into more formal institutions or in the wider community, building social networks and cohesion. A study for example examining black and minority ethnic organisations in Leicester found evidence of community organisation participants gaining experience as management committee members which could then act as a springboard for further community participation. Research on the contribution of faith groups has found that they can contribute to communities by acting as a catalyst for the formation of networks, as welfare service providers, as participants in partnership structures and as a basis for a community coming together around a particular issue.

---

[3] Consultation on the Community Assets Fund, Cabinet Office, March 2007.

[4] Long-term challenges and opportunities for the UK: analysis for the 2007 Comprehensive Spending Review, HM Treasury, 2006

[5] Improving small scale grant funding for local voluntary and community organisations, Discussion paper, Young Foundation, March 2007

3.9 The available evidence therefore confirms the contribution that community organisations can make to building social capital, which may have a further range of potential economic benefits. Community activity and volunteering can for example boost the employment aspirations of individuals, providing the space for skills development in a setting where people can feel confident and empowered. Community activity can contribute to job creation and small business development in a local area. Hidden economic effects of a strong community sector and community activity can also be found to lie within the provision of informal services by the sector, potentially reducing the demand on formal statutory services and the contribution that volunteers make to service provision and support, equivalent to over 1 million full-time workers.

Box 3.2 Partnerships between the state and the local third sector – international perspectives

To contribute to the evidence base for the third sector review, the experiences of different countries' approaches to engaging with small community organisations has been explored, offering interesting lessons for England. Some key examples are highlighted below:

Denmark – the third sector in Denmark is characterised by a relatively high level of volunteerism and a large number of local community associations (around one for every 82 citizens). Public support for small groups is divided amongst three levels of administration – the central government, county councils and municipal councils, with small groups typically funded at the municipal level alongside profits from the national lottery and football pools. Support for third sector organisations is based on a number of values, including independence, decentralisation, cultural democracy and the arms length principle. This principle means that government does not distribute funds directly; instead, independent peer groups of experts and professionals (e.g. the Danish Youth Council) make funding decisions. Moreover, it is rare that grants provided are tied to achieving a particular outcome reducing monitoring requirements.

Australia - A recent snapshot of the third sector shows that there are roughly 700,000 not-for-profit organisations in Australia, most of which are small community organisations, entirely dependent on the voluntary commitment of members. Approximately 35,000 employ staff. In 1999-2000, 30 per cent of sector income was derived from Government grants and contracts.[6] The third sector in Australia is also characterised by high levels of volunteering and membership. In 2004, 6.3 million Australians (41 per cent of the adult population) volunteered a total of 750 million hours for not-for-profit organisations.

There are a multitude of grants available for small community and voluntary organisations. Grants can be distributed by national and federal governments, often through boards and councils (such as the Australia Council for the Arts). In order to enable organisations to find information about grants and programmes, the Commonwealth government has developed a website portal, www.grantslink.gov.au, which breaks down the information into policy areas.

---

[6] Non-profit Institutions Satellite Account, Australian National Accounts 1999/2000, Australian Bureau of Statistics, 2002

3.10 Larger community based social enterprises which often own or manage assets can also have a unique role in building and strengthening communities, acting as an anchor in the community for the provision of services and facilities for the rest of the community sector as well as generating wealth for the community, as set out in paragraph 3.24.

Foundations for a new strategy

3.11 Building on the consultation and this evidence gathered during the third sector review, the Government is proposing a new strategy for building stronger and more active communities through investment in a thriving community sector and community activity and volunteering. The primary responsibility for strengthening communities lies with Local Government, and over the coming years it will be critical that Local Authorities continue to build on the principles of Local Compacts and the Local Government White Paper to develop relationships with the third sector. To support this work, the Government will also make several strategic investments to build the environment to enable community based organisations to thrive and to work with Local Authorities and other local statutory bodies.

3.12 The strategy therefore contains the following mutually reinforcing elements:

- work to further build relationships between the local third sector and Local Authorities;

- investment to improve the level and quality of small grant funding available to community groups;

- investment in community anchors to enable greater enterprise and sustainability;

- continued investment in building a culture of volunteering and mentoring; and,

- capacity building - investing in provision to support smaller community based organisations and volunteers.

Effective local engagement and representation

3.13 Local Authorities have a responsibility for well being in a local area, working with partners to build strong and prosperous communities. The majority of interaction between the third sector and Government is at a local level and the Government has recognised that, while there is clear evidence of good practice in the relationship between the local third sector and local statutory bodies, this practice is inconsistent. Published in October 2006, the Local Government White Paper recognises that the third sector is key to delivering the ambitions to strengthen local accountability, shape places and design and deliver user focused local services.[7] Over the next ten years, the Government wants the best local partnership working to be the rule, not the exception. The paper contains the following key proposals:

---

[7] Strong and Prosperous communities, The Local Government White Paper, DCLG, 2006.

- ensuring the third sector is represented on Local Strategic Partnerships (LSPs), their thematic partnerships and in developing Local Area Agreements (LAAs). Local Strategic Partnerships will bring together the third sector with the public and private sectors to coordinate the contribution that each can make to improve localities. Sustainable Communities Strategies produced by LSPs will provide a framework to promote a strong and healthy local third sector;

- local bodies will be able to utilise themselves and help local people use many of the empowerment provisions in the White Paper; such as Community Calls for Action and Neighbourhood Charters; and,

- providing for stable, sustainable and fair funding by setting a clear expectation through statutory guidance that the starting point for grant funding will be three years unless it does not represent best value in individual cases.

3.14   It is clear that there is a need for Local Authorities to continue to build their partnerships with local third sector organisations, embedding third sector representation into local decision making arenas and providing support for build the capacity of the sector. To support this, Communities and Local Government (CLG) have been working with third sector umbrella bodies to discuss principles of representation to assist the sector in organising itself to strengthen involvement in Local Strategic Partnerships and public life.

3.15   Through the 2007 CSR process, the current sets of local government performance indicators will be replaced by a new, single, performance framework for Local Authorities working alone or in partnership with quantitative areas for improvement in both national and local priorities articulated in the Local Area Agreements. The Office of the Third Sector and CLG are exploring how best the contribution of third sector organisations at a local level can be reflected in this new performance framework for Local Authorities. As set out in their third sector strategy, published in June 2007, CLG are also working with the Audit Commission to develop proposals for Comprehensive Area Assessments that judge the effectiveness of local partnership working, including the involvement of the third sector.[8]

3.16   The Government is also committed to looking at new ways to further strengthen the ability of citizens to influence local decisions. This includes considering introducing a duty requiring Local Authorities to consider and investigate petitions from local communities, provision for local communities to apply for devolved or delegated budgets which will benefit the local community and supporting citizens to contribute to public decision making.[9]

---

[8] Third Sector Strategy for Communities and Local Government, Discussion Paper, Communities and Local Government, June 2007.

[9] The Governance of Britain, HM Government, July 2007.

Box 3.3 Best practice at the local level

The relationship between the local third sector and Local Government is vital. To support the development of this partnership a Local Government/VCS working group came together in 2006 to set out a joint aspiration of what a good relationship at the local level looks like. The working group included the Local Government Association (LGA), the Improvement and Development Agency (IDeA), the Local Government Information Unit (LGIU), the Cabinet Office, the National Association for Voluntary and Community Action (NAVCA), Urban Forum, and the National Council for Voluntary Organisations (NCVO).

The vision sets out areas of good practice in three key areas:

Community engagement, including mainstreaming the principles of the Compact, promoting the development and meaningful application of a Statement of Community Involvement for use in Local Strategic Partnerships, Sustainable Community Strategies, Neighbourhood agreements and Local Area Agreements and promoting the role of the sector in the scrutiny function of Local Government

Social capital and civil renewal, including promoting capacity building in the sector and promoting mechanisms that facilitate networking, representation and participation.

Service delivery, including promoting clarity around the circumstances when grants, service level agreements or contracts are most appropriate, proportionate monitoring and bureaucracy around funding agreements, developing communication systems which provide accessible information on procurement opportunities for the sector and providing appropriate support for organisations to participate in Local Strategic Partnerships.

www.urbanforum.org.uk

Funding the local third sector

3.17   The consultation highlighted that securing funding is the key concern of community based organisations and that the wind down of some grant funding streams such as the Single Regeneration Budget poses particular challenges for some organisations. The report of the Local Community Sector Taskforce recognised that the effects of this wind down have been partially mitigated by new funding programmes, the continuation of regeneration based funding and investment by the Regional Development Agencies and Local Authorities through Local Area Agreements.[10] However, while there are a large number of grants available to organisations there is evidence of increasing competition for that provision and that many organisations lack the capacity to seek funding from a wide variety of different sources.

Principles for funding   **3.18**   Evaluations of different funding sources available to the community sector highlight the positive impact that small grant funding streams can have, leading to innovative work and direct impacts in areas such as boosting skills, increasing confidence and participation, providing resources for communities, strengthening networks and cooperation in a local area. The Young Foundation study indicates that funding approaches that have been successful combine elements of extensive local knowledge, a combination of financial and practical or capacity building support,

---

[10] Local Community Sector Taskforce, December 2006. The Local Community Sector Taskforce was an independent group, reporting to Government. They were commissioned to ensure that central, regional and local government put in place a framework which allows neighbourhood and community groups to manage the wind-down of the Single Regeneration Budget and to ensure there are opportunities for them to access the range of substantial sums of Government investment available.

straightforward application procedures and transparency about the application and funding processes.

3.19   There is also value in maintaining and supporting a mix of grant funding streams from different providers within and outside of local and central Government, ensuring choice for organisations and different options to meet the variety of needs and priorities on both sides of the funding relationship. What is needed is better information and capacity building at a local level to ensure that groups have the relevant advice and support to be able to seek appropriate funding.

Small grants   **3.20**   Over the 2007 CSR years, the Government wants to put in place a strategy to complement and build sustainability into existing provision of grant funding to the sector, which is principally provided by Local Authorities and their partners. Recognising the concerns heard through the consultation, Budget 2007 announced that an £80 million fund would be made available, over four years to provide core funding to grass roots community organisations supporting community action and voice. This funding is designed to complement existing provision by Local Authorities. The funding will be available to all types of community groups including faith and equalities groups representing marginalised communities such as disability groups, women's groups, black and minority ethnic communities and lesbian, gay, bisexual and transgender communities. The funding will be distributed via a variety of local grant funders such as Community Foundations. Local funders bring a variety of benefits to grant distribution:

- they often aggregate different sources of community sector funding, from charitable, private sector and statutory sources, reducing administration costs, promoting value for money and simplifying application processes for community groups;

- many have experience of delivering central government programmes, such as the Local Network Fund on behalf of the Department for Children, Schools and Families; and,

- they have significant local expertise and work with Local Authorities and local third sector infrastructure organisations and other large community organisations in developing appropriate local strategies combining financial and practical support. They are particularly linked into the local area through their frequent use of volunteer panels for grant giving.

3.21   Further details on the small grants programme, including on the nature of the grants available and the mechanisms for distribution will be available shortly.

3.22   Complementing this provision, further small grant support for local third sector organisations will be provided over the 2007 CSR years from sources such as the Big Lottery Fund and the European Social Fund. The Big Lottery Fund has committed to maintaining its current portfolio of programmes and to honour the allocation of 60-70 per cent of its budget to the third sector in cash terms and extend this allocation up to 2012. The EU Structural Funds (the European Social Fund and the European Regional Development Fund) have played an important role in strengthening communities, particularly through improving employment opportunities. The Government expects that the European Social Fund will maintain current levels of provision for small grants (currently provided through the Global grants programme) through the 2007 CSR years.

Building sustainability in local grant making

3.23   Putting additional resources into a small grants programme will over the 2007 CSR years provide much needed support to hundreds of community groups that are helping to build communities. To ensure that this support can be continued into the future the Government will also make available £50 million in capital grants to local independent foundations to invest in endowment funds, which will generate income to be allocated to frontline organisations. This funding will act as a catalyst for drawing in other sources of funding to a local area from the private sector and as such will be allocated on a match-funded basis with charitable and corporate contributions. Funding to build local endowments will begin in April 2008.

Box 3.4 Community endowments in Northern Ireland

The Community Foundation for Northern Ireland is a good example of how endowment funding from Government can lever in additional corporate and charitable donations to build sustainability for future grant provision.

Established in 1979, the Community Foundation for Northern Ireland is an independent grant-making organisation. It manages a broad portfolio of funds and programmes that address social exclusion, poverty and social injustice.

The Community Foundation for Northern Ireland celebrated its 25th anniversary in 2004. In recognition of this milestone, the Government pledged a £3 million Challenge Grant to consolidate the endowment base of the Foundation. This Challenge Grant from the Department for Social Development was offered on condition that the Community Foundation matched the amount of money pledged on a £1 for £1 basis.

An independent charitable donor, Atlantic Philanthropies, committed £2 million and a further £1.4 million was raised from other private sources – more than matching the Challenge Grant and doubling the Foundation's endowment.

Investment in community anchors

3.24   Community anchors are large neighbourhood based organisations playing a vital role in generating wealth for communities and in supporting other community sector organisations. They are often social enterprises, able to generate income through trading and contracting, often through ownership or management of an asset base. They play a unique role, recognised within communities and by external agencies and able to act as an intermediate between these agencies and grassroots activity. They can deliver services beyond the capacity of smaller groups, operate as a platform for community activity, facilitate wider community forums and networks and can negotiate on behalf of the local community sector. They also contribute to wealth creation in an area, by investing in the personal development of individuals, which can connect people to the labour market and by improving benefit take-up and reducing outgoings through advocacy and advice. In addition, they contribute to the wealth of the community by providing services that reduce the transaction costs of the public sector and by generating their own income, by a variety of methods they ensure that wealth is retained in an area.[11]

---

[11] For a fuller discussion of the role of community anchor type organisations the Government's strategy for community capacity building Firm Foundations, 2004 provides an overview, building on academic research such as: Building communities, changing lives. The contribution of large, independent neighbourhood regeneration organisations, Stephen Thake for the Joseph Rowntree Foundation, 2001.

3.25 The thematic roundtable discussion on strengthening communities highlighted that the provision of small grants to the community sector needed to go hand in hand with the development of community anchors to build strong and sustainable communities.[12] The roundtable discussion suggested five key priorities for community anchor organisations as providing a place to meet and for community activities to take place, to support and promote the growth of the wider community sector, to provide services, to provide advocacy and voice for the community and to stimulate community involvement and activity.

3.26 Firm Foundations, which sets out the Government's framework for community capacity building, includes the development and support of community anchor organisations as a key driver of community building.[13] Government support for this activity has included funding for the Community Alliance organisations[14] to develop the community anchor approach and investment in the Adventure Capital Fund (ACF) as a source of funds for social enterprise based community anchor organisations. More recently the Big Lottery Fund infrastructure programme, BASIS has announced investment of £3.1 million for the Community Alliance for a five-year regional programme to enable the Alliance to provide a single point of contact in the regions for community groups to access information and services to improve their governance and strategic planning and to become more sustainable and effective.

3.27 The Adventure Capital Fund has been successful in investing over £5 million in patient capital in community based organisations, since its inception in 2002. Evaluation of round one of the ACF has indicated that there is a significant level of demand for this type of funding, with round one funding oversubscribed fivefold on the patient capital side.[15] In addition, the selection process precipitated organisational and cultural change within the organisations involved, particularly around moving away from grant funding reliance to developing independence and sustainability through enterprise. Round two evaluation confirmed the demand for long-term loan finance for community-based organisations developing revenue earning enterprise initiatives, however it is also clear that organisations require support (which the ACF provides through its Supporters network) to build capacity. [16] The evaluation found that patient capital investment of this type is particularly relevant for organisations with a turnover between £100,000 and £1million, with few significant capital assets or revenue surpluses and organisations with turnovers in excess of £1million but with low trading surpluses and a need for asset development.

Assets **3.28** Government investment in asset development, as set out in paragraphs 3.4-3.5 also plays a vital role in building the sustainability of community anchor organisations. Following on from the recommendations and findings of the Quirk Review of community management and ownership of assets, the Government has committed to implement the proposals in full. [17] The Government will work with third sector partners to: raise awareness of the Review's findings; to demonstrate how asset transfer can be done; to strengthen community capacity to use the powers available to them to create pressure for asset transfer; to develop resources to support asset development; and, to

---

[12] Held in York, in February 2007 and chaired by the Archbishop of York, Dr John Sentamu.

[13] Firm Foundations, The Government's Framework for Community Capacity Building, Home Office, 2004.

[14] Community Matters, Bassac and the Development Trusts Association.

[15] Primed for Growth. Adventure Capital Fund Baseline Report. Stephen Thake.

[16] Adventure Capital Fund Round 2. Baseline Report: defining the market. Stephen Thake November 2005.

[17] Opening the transfer window. The Government's response to the Quirk Review of community management and ownership of public assets, Communities and Local Government, May 2007.

promote the benefits of community management or ownership of assets. In July 2007, 20 Local Authorities were selected to be involved in the Advancing Assets for Communities programme, funded by CLG, which will demonstrate how Local Authorities and community organisations can be supported to develop joint plans for asset transfer in line with the recommendations of the Quirk Review.

Clawback **3.29** Revised *Guidance to funders*, issued in May 2006, takes account of a HM Treasury review in 2005 about the operation of the clawback rule and how it could work more flexibly.[18] When providing funds for the purposes of acquiring or developing an asset, funding bodies should, where appropriate, retain a financial interest in the asset. However, while it is correct to safeguard taxpayers' interests, Government should still be pragmatic and realistic in setting charges. Conditions should therefore be flexible, and not create barriers to wider policy objectives. **There is a strong expectation, for example, that funders automatically drop clawback provisions older than 10 years - or indeed less if the objective itself has already been met. Community groups should also generally be permitted to retain income that they generate from the asset, for example through hire.**

3.30 The Government acknowledges that to make the rules easier to use in practice, the attitudes and practice of funders will need to change. Currently, funders tend to consider clawback in relation to individual grants, but **the Government will consider how general clawback conditions might apply to a whole programme or on a thematic or category basis; or whether it is appropriate to articulate levels below which it may not be cost-effective for funders to apply clawback.**

3.31 Following the report of the Quirk Review, CLG will work with the Office of the Third Sector and HM Treasury to encourage central Government departments, Local Authorities, and other public bodies to review their approach to clawback. CLG in partnership with the Local Government Association (LGA) and Government Offices (GOs) will furthermore initiate a high profile 3-year campaign on community management and ownership of assets based on raising awareness. Finally, CLG, the Audit Commission, the Chartered Institute of Public Finance and Accountancy (CIPFA) and the LGA will together publish comprehensive, up-to-date and authoritative guidance on Local Authority asset management with specific guidance on clawback.

3.32 Building on existing investment and work the CLG third sector strategy sets out a commitment to examine an approach to supporting community anchors over the 2007 CSR years.[19] In particular, **CLG are consulting on an approach focusing on supporting community anchors to stimulate and develop self-sufficiency through asset management and ownership and through expansion of earned revenue. The Office of the Third Sector will also commit over the 2007 CSR years £10 million to support the development of community anchor organisations.** Subject to decisions in the 2007 CSR this package of funding and support will represent a new commitment to support sustainability and enterprise in the community sector. The CLG consultation ends on 20 September 2007.

---

[18] Improving financial relationships with the third sector: Guidance to funders and purchasers, HM Treasury, May 2006.

[19] Third Sector Strategy for Communities and Local Government. Discussion Paper, Communities and Local Government, June 2007.

Building a culture of volunteering and mentoring

3.33   As set out in the interim report of the third sector review, the contribution that volunteers make to strengthening communities, supporting others, protecting the environment and building civil society is enormous. In 2005, over 20 million people in England volunteered formally or informally at least once a month, representing half the adult population.[20] Voluntary activity is vital in supporting the range of activity undertaken by third sector organisations and within the public services, with volunteers acting as magistrates, special constables and school governors, amongst other things. Strong communities, empowered to achieve change, would not be able to do so without the contribution of volunteers while mentoring and other forms of mutual support provided by volunteers can be as valuable as professional support for individuals.

3.34   Government investment in volunteering and mentoring has been significant and is built upon the rationale that:

- volunteering is not a free good for organisations, and often investment is required for recruiting, training and managing volunteers;

- there are individual level barriers to active participation, including lack of suitable opportunities, perceived lack of time and, as the third sector review consultation demonstrated, perceived public policy barriers around the need for Criminal Records Bureau checks in some instances and misunderstanding around the rules around volunteering whilst on benefits; and,

- there are significant benefits to promoting voluntary activity at the level of the individual (for example increased confidence, skills building for later employment, developing networks), the community and wider society.

3.35   Over the next ten years the Government wants to continue working to build a culture of volunteering and will make investments over the 2007 CSR years to provide the platform for further growth in voluntary activity.

---

[20] 2005 Citizenship Survey, DCLG, June 2006.

Box 3.5 Mentoring

Mentoring is the support of one individual by another in a relationship developed through regular contact over a period of time, in order to achieve a stated objective. It can take a number of forms – traditionally mentoring is a relationship between an adult and a younger or more vulnerable person facing a period of difficulty, but recent innovations include peer mentoring, which involves on young person providing support to another young person often in their school, and e-mentoring which describes support given through email and chat across the internet.

The Government has supported peer mentoring through the national pilot, which is working in 180 secondary schools to build the evidence of what works in reducing bullying, raising attainment and easing transitions.

Mentoring can have a beneficial effect on young people in disadvantaged situations, such as young people growing up in poverty, with difficult family situations or with behavioural difficulties. Although mentoring is a relatively expensive activity (traditional forms of face to face mentoring can cost between £2000 to £5000 per year), in some cases it is the only real way to reach the most disadvantaged children. Traditional forms of mentoring can improve engagement in education, employment and training, tackle anger and violence and reduce drug use. Although the evidence base is less developed regarding peer mentoring and e-mentoring, the former may reduce bullying, improve attainment and integrate pupils better into school life (and the benefits for the mentors may be as great as for the mentees), and the latter can provide young people with valuable guidance about their futures.[21]

Horsesmouth is an e-mentoring website initiative, funded by practical learning foundation Edge and **v**, ready to provide thousands of new volunteering opportunities for young people. Based on a social networking model the site is a free, enjoyable and secure environment in which anyone aged 16 or over can give time through informal e-mentoring. There are a collection of unique tools that mentors can use including: profiling their experiences, publishing their pearls of wisdom, managing and counting their volunteer mentoring time, and sharing interesting weblinks and inspiring books via their library. In addition, the site features a "reputation system" called the M-factor, which allows members to rate their mentors on their friendliness, and the usefulness and speed of their response. The Horsesmouth community is growing swiftly and will be celebrating with a formal launch this summer.

3.36   Patterns of behaviour are most strongly developed when people are young, yet young people feel they lack the knowledge on how to get involved and act on their passionate concerns about global and local issues.[22] The Government has already invested in the new, independent organisation, **v**, to begin to build a new national youth volunteering framework. [23] **v** is led by the cares, passions, interests and beliefs of young people through **v20**, its Youth Advisory Board. Progress is good, with **v** commissioning over 120,000 volunteering opportunities in its first year and launching an innovative youth fund (vcashpoint), developed by **v20**, that will give young volunteers the chance to apply for up to £2500 to run voluntary community projects. **v** has also launched vinspired.com, a new youth volunteering portal, and an awareness campaign on the theme "whatsyourv?". **v**'s operations sit alongside significant investments made in broader youth services as set out in the ten year youth strategy.

---

[21] Lean on Me: Mentoring for young people at risk – a guide for donors and funders; New Philanthropy Capital, May 2007.

[22] Barriers preventing passionate young people acting on their concerns, v, June 2007.

[23] The Russell Commission report, published in March 2005 made 16 recommendations to build a framework and a culture of youth volunteering, which the Government committed to implement in full. v is the independent organisation set up to take forward many of the recommendations in the report.

3.37   Over the 2007 CSR years, the Government will invest around £117 million in v, which includes funding for the successor to the previous Millennium Volunteers programme for young people. The Government will in addition maintain the arrangement where it matches contributions from private businesses for the youth volunteering agenda. **v** has already attracted pledges totalling £21 million from a diverse range of private sector organisations under this match funding scheme, leading to some highly innovative projects and partnership working.

3.38   With this investment, **v** will deliver:

- greater awareness of volunteering among young people, through campaigns and the newly launched vinspired.com portal; and, through research, a greater understanding of what young people want;

- a total of 300,000 opportunities, including through a new National Youth Volunteering Programme which will bring greater coherence and consistency by combining the best of Millennium Volunteers with the creation of new opportunities and a national framework for recognition and awards; and,

- significant investment from private sector organisations in order to achieve these goals.

Volunteering in the public services   **3.39**   Many opportunities for volunteering for both young people and adults lie in key areas of public services delivery. The Office of the Third Sector working with the Government's new Volunteering Champion, Baroness Julia Neuberger, will work with Government Departments and their agencies, to ensure that they have plans in place to engage a wide range of volunteers in the work of Departments, recognising that the contribution of volunteers to the direct delivery of public services and to wider public policy goals can be critical.

Employee volunteering   **3.40**   Almost one quarter of employees across the country work for an employer with a scheme for volunteering.[24] The Government believes that the public sector is well placed to act in a leadership role in driving employee volunteering to become the norm, by raising the quantity, quality and profile of employee volunteering across the public sector.

3.41   A number of Government Departments give an entitlement to participate in any voluntary activity, whereas others give discretionary paid leave for voluntary activities that the Department believes contribute to or are closely aligned with its objectives, while others have a mixed economy of the two. The Cabinet Office, working with Baroness Julia Neuberger, will also take forward work to drive through improvements in the quantity and quality of employee volunteering in the public sector, particularly through allowing staff clear entitlements to undertake voluntary activity, and through taking active steps to promote volunteering amongst staff.

---

[24] 2005 Citizenship Survey, DCLG, June 2006.

Boosting existing investments in volunteering

3.42 The Government will also continue to invest in promoting volunteering opportunities and breaking down the barriers to volunteering, particularly for socially excluded groups. The Volunteering for All programme which aims to boost participation among groups who do not volunteer as much as others will continue into the 2007 CSR years. This will be combined with the current GoldStar programme which invests in promoting best practice in volunteering and mentoring in order to scale up projects that are delivering real benefits to communities. In recognition of the importance of voluntary activity in building trust in communities and promoting community cohesion, the Government will also make available, within this new combined programme, funding to build capacity in intergenerational volunteering.

Volunteer training

3.43 Although there is a wide variety of training programmes available for volunteers and volunteer managers, provision can be patchy and standards vary depending on the nature of volunteering and the volunteer involving organisation concerned. The Cabinet Office will work with the Commission for the Future of Volunteering, and in consultation with other key stakeholders, to take forward the best way of enabling enhanced and more widespread training for volunteers and those working with volunteers.

Box 3.6 Community engagement and social enterprise through cooperative structures

In 1999, the Football Task Force recommended a number of measures to enable supporters to become more involved in the running and future of their clubs.

In response, the Government launched Supporters Direct, one of whose functions is to "promote and support the concept of democratic supporter ownership and representation through mutual, not-for-profit structures". The preferred structure is the Community Benefit Society registered under the Industrial and Provident Societies Act 1965. There are now over 140 Supporters Trusts, 78 of which hold equity in their clubs. Of those 78, 12 hold more than half of the equity and thus describe their clubs as "supporter owned", and one controls the club with the support of the shareholders.

The Supporters Trust for Brentford FC is the Brentford Football Community Society Ltd (known as "Bees United") and has in excess of 1600 members. Bees United owns a majority (60 per cent) shareholding in Brentford FC and aims to:

- strengthen bonds between the club and the local community;

- promote football as a focus for community involvement and engagement;

- provide and maintain facilities for professional football; and,

- promote inclusive coaching schemes (such as schemes for Asian players, for young women, and for disabled players).

Hounslow Borough Council contributed £0.5m of the £6m that Bees United needed to raise to buy the majority shareholding. Bees United are clear that the Council's decision to contribute was directly attributable to the community ownership of Bees United and of the high priority they give to community involvement. For example, under Bees United's ownership the club:

- hosts the Brentford FC Community Sports Trust, a registered charity whose aim is to encourage community participation in sport, for the health and social welfare benefits that it brings to participants. The Trust has 50 qualified sports coaches working in the local community all year round and attracts over 30,000 young people every year into its programmes .

- hosts the Griffin Park Learning Zone, which uses sports as a way of improving literacy, numeracy and IT skills in 7-14 year olds. In 2005-06 over 300 children from 17 Hounslow schools participated in the programme at Griffin Park.

The club has been at Griffin Park for over 100 years and now seeks to build a new stadium nearby. The new stadium, to be built on a brownfield site, is intended to act as a vibrant community hub as well as providing a 20,000-seat arena for football, rugby and potentially other sports. The plans for it include:

- an indoor sports centre, to be run by the local authority;

- a health centre accommodating GPs, dentists, physiotherapists etc;

- a social enterprise business centre;

- an education zone along the lines of the Griffin Park Learning Zone; and

- housing, hotel and leisure facilities that will provide an income for the club.

Community capacity building

3.44   Community capacity building is the encouragement and provision of practical support to people to act together voluntarily to tackle problems, influence public services, meet social needs and improve the quality of life in their communities.[25] Community capacity building is concerned with the resources of the population in question, both as already expressed in existing groups and as potential for greater involvement by people who are not already participating. The kinds of activities that might encompass community capacity building therefore include helping new community groups establish, helping groups to identify needs within their communities, providing information and advice, assisting with fundraising, facilitating consultation, providing training, advocacy and community representation.

3.45   Community capacity building is delivered through various channels, including through local infrastructure organisations, community anchor organisations as described above and community development workers, often employed by the Local Authority (around 42 per cent of workers) and in the sector itself, with estimates suggesting that there are around 15-20,000 full-time equivalent community capacity building workers, concentrated in regeneration areas.[26] In rural areas, Rural Community Councils, County Associations of Local Councils, County Training Partnerships and Parish Councils often provide capacity building support. Government support for community building activity is therefore largely delivered by Local Authorities, but also through national programmes such as ChangeUp, delivered by Capacitybuilders, support for community anchors and through national funding programmes for rural communities, including the Rural Social and Community Programme and programmes that support Quality Parishes and Parish Planning. Local Authority focused Government funded programmes for rural areas include Rural Excellence which provides mentoring between rural Local Authorities, the 7th Beacon programme which celebrates and promotes Local Authority rural service delivery, and Rural Pathfinders which encourage innovative approaches to rural services.

3.46   Alongside the development of community anchors the Government, over the 2007 CSR years, wants to make further improvements to the capacity of local infrastructure organisations to reach small community based organisations. **As set out in Chapter 6, the Government is committed to future investment in infrastructure support to the third sector through Capacitybuilders. Over the 2007 CSR years, this support will be increasingly focused on ensuring that infrastructure organisations are able to support the local community sector and have the capacity to reach into the smallest and most marginalised communities. Capacitybuilders will also invest £5 million in capital over the CSR years in a modernised volunteering and third sector infrastructure as part of the overall investment in capacity building and support.**

---

[25] Who are the capacity builders? A study of provision for strengthening the role of local communities, Peter Taylor, Community Development Foundation, 2006.

[26] As above

4 TRANSFORMING PUBLIC SERVICES

Summary

The Government recognises the vital role that some organisations play in the design and delivery of public services.

The Government will:

- invest in training for the commissioners of public services so they are aware of the different providers available to them;

- continue to work with commissioners pioneering the use of social clauses;

- support Local Authorities to assess the quality of their relationships with the third sector;

- commission a study into the potential role of third sector organisations in delivering employment services;

- engage in further work to understand the relationship between demand-led funding and funding for the third sector;

- identify key opportunities for third sector organisations to deliver more and better public services; and,

- invest £65 million in the Futurebuilders Fund, providing loans and grants to organisations looking to deliver public services in all areas.

INTRODUCTION

4.1 The third sector has historically played an important role in providing public services, identifying needs, campaigning for change and developing dynamic, innovative solutions. Social enterprises often, in addition, combine a business approach to the provision of key public services. The best organisations are typified by a strong focus on the needs of service users; knowledge and expertise to meet complex personal needs and tackle difficult social issues; an ability to be flexible, offer joined-up service delivery and with the experience to innovate. The third sector's often close relationships with the users of its services enables it to promote 'co-production' of outcomes, where users are equal partners with professionals in transforming services to suit their needs. By functioning as intermediaries between people and public services, third sector organisations can often improve the interaction between the two. This can help to drive innovation, to give people a democratic voice and to enable active citizenship. The third sector can also promote accountability, by providing a challenge and advocacy role on behalf of citizens at the margins of society.

4.2 The Government therefore wants to continue to ensure that the third sector remains at the heart of measures to improve public services including as contractors delivering public services, as campaigners for change, as advisers influencing the design of services and as innovators from which the public sector can learn.

4.3   The earlier cross-cutting Government reviews in the 2002 and 2004 Spending Reviews focused on the role of the sector in public service delivery and improvement. They began to identify specific advantages the sector can bring to delivery and recognised that it can improve services by being involved in design, commissioning and evaluation. However, they also recognised that barriers preventing more extensive involvement had first to be tackled and called for improved awareness of the benefits of the sector among policymakers at both a national and local level. The Action Plan for Third Sector Public Service Delivery sets out a blueprint on how all third sector organisations can be better involved in a public services partnership by focusing action on the issues of commissioning and procurement, innovation, and accountability.[1]

THE CONSULTATION

4.4   The interim report of the third sector review highlighted the key themes from the consultation including that:

- there remains a gap between the Government's ambition to increase the third sector's involvement in public services and the experience of frontline organisations – particularly at the local level;

- there is inconsistency in the commissioning and procurement practices of some statutory bodies. Both the public and third sectors need to better understand the commissioning and procurement process, as well as issues around fairer funding and proportionate risk management;

- Government must consider the wider part the sector can play in shaping and designing services, as well as delivery. The narrow focus on financial efficiency and value for money of some public funders is also causing unintended consequences for the sector's ability to truly transform services. Commissioners must acknowledge and understand this, recognising wider social gains, and acknowledging broader outcomes;

- larger contracts may present a problem or an opportunity – depending on how they are approached. More work needs to be done on the issue of sub-contracting, acknowledging that organisations act in a competitive market, but with consideration on how risk and burdens are shared between parties;

- better evidence is needed to understand the interaction in the relationship between the public and third sector; the value of the engagement with the citizen and in complex problems; and the nature of innovation; and,

- a clearer definition is needed from Government of what it wants the sector to measure, and be measured by, so that information can be collected systematically, proportionally, and be better used – with feedback to providers on quality.

4.5   The interim report of the third sector review set out that the Government would continue to build the evidence base on the role of the third sector in public service delivery to support the implementation of the Action Plan for Third Sector Public Service Delivery. As set out in Box 4.1, the Action Plan is responding to many concerns arising from consultation and focuses particularly on improving the day-to-day experiences of third sector organisations working with front-line commissioners and

---

[1] Partnership in Public Services: an Action Plan for Third Sector Involvement, Cabinet Office, December 2006.

procurement officers. Going forward, it provides the foundation which the Government will continue to build on in order to transform public services through more effective working with the third sector.

THE FUTURE ROLE OF THE THIRD SECTOR IN TRANSFORMING PUBLIC SERVICES

4.6 The 2004 Spending Review document: *Exploring the role of the third sector in public service delivery and reform* set out an analytical framework for the potential benefits of third sector public service delivery including: [2]

- a strong focus on the needs of service users;

- knowledge and expertise to meet complex personal needs and tackle difficult social issues;

- an ability to be flexible and offer joined-up service delivery;

- the capacity to build users' trust; and,

- the experience and independence to innovate.

4.7 Alongside wider benefits from:

- involving local people to build community ownership;

- building the skills and experience of volunteers;

- increasing trust within and across communities, thereby building social capital.

Varney review **4.8** More recently, Sir David Varney's review on Service Transformation, published alongside the 2006 Pre-Budget Report, emphasises the Government's commitment to improving the ways citizens and businesses are able to contact Government and receive services.[3] It notes that the Government has already recognised the value of the third sector, but acknowledges the need for the "centre and Local Government to work together to facilitate and increase substantially the use of third sector intermediaries in improving public services." Potential benefits include:

- greater engagement with the current and potential service user in the design and delivery of services, with public service organisations actively seeking the views of the customer on the services on offer;

- improved service delivery, including greater tailoring of the service to the needs of the individual, greater speed of service, greater accuracy of re-using data already supplied and verified, more convenient access to services, and new services;

- more consistent quality of government services as a result of joined up working and benchmarking in operation and strategy; and,

- efficiency benefits by finding more cost effective and less duplicative ways of working as well as more effective early intervention strategies.

---

[2] Exploring the Role of the Third Sector in Public Service Delivery and Reform: a Discussion Document, HM Treasury, February 2005.

[3] Service Transformation: A better service for citizens and businesses, a better deal for the taxpayer, December 2006.

4.9 There is an opportunity for Government to learn from these third sector innovations and disseminate their lessons across public service delivery. Some critical factors for ongoing sustainability identified from successful projects include the need to have clear objectives; ensure best value for money, and staff motivation; achieve a shared vision and "buy-in" to any change from every level involved in the process; and the need to organise service delivery around the customer. The recommendations of the Varney review are being taken forward through the Service Transformation Delivery Plan, which is being developed under the leadership of Sir Gus O'Donnell, the Cabinet Secretary, and will be published alongside the 2007 CSR.

Supporting the multiple roles of the third sector **4.10** The Government recognises the multiple roles of the sector in transforming public services: in delivery, as a partner in innovation; as a partner in the design of services and as campaigner for change in the way services are delivered. Over the next ten years, the Government wants to build the environment so that the third sector can play an increasingly important contribution to the design and delivery of better services and outcomes for users by:

- improving the commissioning and procurement landscape;

- building the evidence on the multiple roles of the third sector in transforming public services;

- working to ensure that the third sector can take advantage of new opportunities and developments in public service reform; and,

- building the capacity of third sector organisations to deliver public services.

Box 4.1 Partnership in Public Services: an action plan for third sector involvement

In December 2006, the Office of the Third Sector, in partnership with five major central Government Departments, published a plan with 18 key actions to improve Government's engagement with the sector in commissioning, procurement, learning from the third sector and accountability. The Social Enterprise Action Plan published in November 2006 also set out measures to enable social enterprises to work with Government, particularly in the delivery and shaping of public services. Key areas of progress include:

- the Improvement and Development Agency is now working with Government departments to ensure that commissioning frameworks reflect the eight core principles set out in the action plan. Departments will report back on progress in September 2007;

- the Improvement and Development Agency has started to develop a National Programme for Third Sector Commissioning, targeted at 2,000 of the most important commissioners with the sector;

- a consortium led by the Innovation Unit have been announced as the delivery partner for the Innovation Exchange, which will be launched in August. The Office of the Third Sector and NESTA have worked together to create a small fund to provide financial and in-kind support to the very best innovations identified by the Innovation Exchange;

- research published by Social Enterprise London on the opportunities for social enterprises in the delivery of the 2012 Olympics;

- the Social Exclusion Task Force are developing a Code of Practice for evaluating public services, aimed at commissioners and providers. The Code will seek to ensure that commissioning decisions are driven by rigorous evidence about what works;

- the Cabinet Office is working with New Philanthropy Capital to measure the administrative burdens associated with public service contracts. This work will help inform departmental simplification plans to reduce burdens on the third sector;

- the Office of the Third Sector is working with the North-East Regional Centre of Excellence to develop a set of model social clauses and to pilot their use; and,

- from April 2008, Futurebuilders funding will be open to all third sector organisations working to deliver public services.

Embedding best practice in commissioning and procurement

4.11   The Government acknowledges the challenge the third sector must face in reconciling the call for financial efficiency and value for money in commissioning public services, as set out by Sir Peter Gershon in his independent review of public sector efficiency, and the opportunity to shape, design, and truly transform those services.[4] Commissioners need to acknowledge and understand the wider social gains, and broader outcomes, that will be achieved by working in partnership with the sector. This will only be achieved if there are concerted efforts at both the national and local level to strengthen the commissioning and procurement framework, and to disseminate good practice.

---

[4] Releasing resource to the frontline. Independent Review of Public Sector Efficiency, Sir Peter Gershon, July 2004.

4.12 · The Action Plan for Third Sector Public Service Delivery sets out a number of concrete measures to set the framework to improve the commissioning and procurement landscape. During the 2007 CSR years the Government will need to work to ensure that these commitments, the training provided for commissioners, and tools such as standard contracts, are fully embedded. At a local level, the Local Government White Paper made a commitment to providing fair, sustainable and stable funding for the third sector.[5] Communities and Local Government are working with the Charted Institute of Public Finance Accountants, the Audit Commission and the Local Government Association to review funding and commissioning practices to set out a more intelligent approach. This will include establishing best practice guidance. Furthermore, the Government will:

- **deliver and extend the National Programme for Third Sector Commissioning.** This will be led by the Improvement and Development Agency (IDeA) in partnership with the Office of the Third Sector and will in the first instance train 2,000 commissioners in Local Authorities, National Offender Management Service, Jobcentre Plus and Primary Care Trusts. **The programme will continue through the 2007 CSR years** and will build in sustainability and long-term change, including through embedding the principles of good commissioning from the start; and,

- continue action to disseminate and embed *Guidance to Funders*, which encourages more flexible longer-term funding and the appropriate sharing of risks, and clarifies the rules on advance payments. [6] **A modernised version of Government Accounting, (*Managing Public Money*,) which provides guidance on a wide variety of issues relating mainly to the proper handling and reporting of public money, will be reissued in July and will include advice on working with the third sector, reiterating the messages already in** *Guidance to Funders*.[7]

4.13 Concerns remain in the sector that the move towards implementing the Gershon report has led to the award of bigger contracts in order to achieve efficiency gains through going to scale and the search for lower transaction costs. This may present a problem or an opportunity for smaller third sector organisations. The Government acknowledges that more work needs to ensure that smaller and specialist organisations are not squeezed out of the delivery market so that the fullest range of organisations are involved in services.

4.14 The Action Plan for Third Sector Public Service Delivery provides an opportunity to better consider how risk and burdens are shared between the funder and provider, the role that might be played through sub-contracting and consortia-building and the incentives to encourage better partnership arrangements and new specialist providers to contribute to the design and delivery of services. These approaches can be mutually beneficial and enable organisations to achieve what would not be possible alone, to address issues strategically, better meet complex needs, create more focused services, and ensure a more powerful voice for users.

Promoting social value **4.15** The value that the sector may bring to public service delivery can also be recognised within the commissioning and procurement process itself and there are a

---

[5] Strong and Prosperous communities, The Local Government White Paper, DCLG, 2006.

[6] Improving Financial Relationships with the Third Sector: Guidance to Funders and Purchasers, HM Treasury, May 2006.

[7] www.government-accounting.gov.uk

range of ways in which an organisation's broader social impacts can already be factored into funding relationships in a way that is consistent with the principles set out through the Gershon review on efficiency. The Action Plan for Third Sector Public Service Delivery and the Social Enterprise Action Plan set out how the Government will consult on tackling barriers to recognising these wider community benefits.

4.16 Examples of existing investment into this work include two projects funded through HM Treasury's Invest to Save Budget. The London Borough of Camden, with the New Economics Foundation is working to develop a new model for commissioning public services from third sector providers that builds economic, social and environmental outcomes into the procurement process. The first findings of the research will be available in the autumn. The Office for National Statistics is looking to establish a tool that service commissioning authorities can use to assess and monitor the performance of public services delivered by third sector organisations in a way directly comparable with public or private sector providers.

4.17 The North-East Regional Centre of Excellence and the Office of the Third Sector are already leading on work to support the development of template social clauses for key service areas through commissioning and procurement frameworks, in order to achieve multiple and joined-up outcomes for citizens. Alongside the Office of Government Commerce, they will continue to work over the 2007 CSR period with commissioners pioneering the use of social clauses and will draw together leading practice.

Local action   **4.18** In the 2005 Pre-Budget Report, the Government announced the development of local area pathfinders, identifying Local Authorities that would commit to the full implementation of the Compact principles and explore ways in which the third sector can add value to the delivery of local services. The December 2006 report sets out the findings of work in Cumbria, Dorset, Nottingham, Portsmouth and Tower Hamlets and summarises key success factors to working with the third sector.[8] These include:

- a strategic commitment to third sector partnership in Sustainable Community Strategies and Local Area Agreements;

- senior member and official level accountability for the delivery of these commitments - supplemented with training and resources;

- regular dialogue, and early involvement with the third sector, in commissioning and decision-making; and,

- institutionalising the Compact funding principles in commissioning and procurement practices.

4.19 In each pathfinder area, an action plan has been produced drawing together the approaches to strengthen the local partnership between the council and the third sector. The Office of the Third Sector will review the results of local area pathfinders and identify ways of spreading the good practices developed by the pathfinders more widely, working with regional and local partners. Building on the progress made in each of these areas and the measures in the Local Government White Paper, over the 2007 CSR years the Government will develop a new local survey of the third sector. The survey will aim to give an indication of both the overall health of the sector in different areas and the quality of relationships with local statutory agencies. It should help Local Authorities, other local public bodies, the sector and the public understand local

---

[8] Local area pathfinders – building public service partnerships, HM Treasury, 2006

strengths and weaknesses and identify areas for progress. The survey design will commence later this summer, aiming for the first survey to be undertaken in later 2008 or early 2009.

Box 4. 2 Supporting People, delivered in partnership

The Supporting People programme helps more than a million people each year to attain or maintain independence, through the provision of housing related support services. Created in 2003, it provides the means through which Government ensures that some of society's most vulnerable people receive help and support to live independently.

The programme was built upon the efforts of voluntary agencies, charities and housing associations over many years. The third sector provides some two-thirds of the services enabled by the Supporting People programme, and receives over £1 billion annually of the funds invested by local authorities in housing support services.

Supporting People already has a strong record in delivering appropriate, personalised services and interventions which are tailored to the needs of individuals. In June 2007, Communities and Local Government published *Independence and Opportunity*, the national strategy for Supporting People, which makes clear that housing support should be part of a coordinated approach to delivering for the most disadvantaged and vulnerable people. [9] Partnership between Local Authorities and their third sector partners is a vital part of making that happen.

The national strategy also set out the commitment that Government will minimise obstacles preventing good quality providers from third sector organisations from competing fairly to deliver housing support services. The Government will also support the third sector as new initiatives such as Local Area Agreements and the personalisation and choice agenda are introduced.

Supporting People continues to support Local Authorities to work intelligently with the third sector through effective commissioning and procurement approaches - through the national Value Improvement programme, which is overseen by a project board that includes third sector representatives.

In addition, the Supporting People programme has provided additional funding to SITRA and the Housing Associations Charitable Trust (HACT) and is working with those umbrella organisations to address capacity building issues, including partnership working and building consortia, to enable third sector providers to deliver effective and efficient services.

Building the evidence

4.20 Since the 2004 Spending Review, there has been some increasing evidence of third sector organisations delivering effective public services. For example, Small Business Service research has highlighted a growing number of social enterprises operating in key public service sectors such as health, education and social care and highlights cases of social enterprises winning contracts against competition from larger companies and then going on to engage in successful service delivery.[10] The report provides strong evidence that social enterprises are willing to "go the extra mile" in terms of motivation and commitment for their users, with levels of service delivery matching that of conventional businesses.

---

[9] Independence and Opportunity, Our strategy for Supporting People, Communities and Local Government, June 2007

[10] A study of the Benefits of Public Sector Procurement from Small Business. SBS Research Report 2005.

4.21   The interim report of the third sector review however, recognised the desire to be able to further demonstrate the third sector's impact in public service delivery more persuasively through a stronger evidence base, moving beyond individual examples of good practice. The thematic roundtable discussion on public services also highlighted that better evidence is needed to understand the value of the engagement of the third sector with the citizen in dealing with complex problems and in the provision of services to them.[11]

The evidence base   **4.22**   There are several reasons why the evidence base is under developed, not least because the question about the third sector's relative effectiveness in delivering public services is relatively recent and the focus of interest is rarely on the type of provider but on the nature of the intervention. Moreover, value added comparisons are difficult to make as the third sector tends to operate in different markets to the private and public sectors, where for example, there is a market failure or the service caters to a client group with very distinct, or individual needs. The third sector also lacks scale relative to both the public and private sectors and tends to operate in local markets. Evidence gathering therefore needs to focus on:

- evidence of the value (i.e. outcomes) that third sector add when they work with the public sector;

- evidence of the value that third sector bring to the actual processes of service delivery (e.g. they bring a greater culture of inclusiveness);

- evidence of distinctive or higher quality end outputs of service delivery - a value for money argument for using the sector; and,

- evidence of the 'distinctive' or comparative value that third sector bring when they work with the public sector (i.e. those things they bring that the public sector can't or generally doesn't).

4.23   As set out in Chapter 6, the Government is committed to investing in improving the evidence base on the third sector overall and this work will include building the evidence on the roles of the sector in public service transformation. With this evidence, the third sector working in partnership with Government will further be able to make the case for improving the landscape for increased involvement of the third sector, including social enterprises, in the design and delivery of services over the next ten years.

4.24   In looking at the options for the future of delivery of welfare to work programmes, the Freud Review published in March 2007, proposed a significant expansion of contestability with proposals to contract with providers to support all long-term benefit claimants into work. As a first step, and in advance of the creation of the new third sector research programme, the Office of the Third Sector will commission a study into the potential role of third sector organisations in the delivery of employment services in order to understand the lessons from successful third sector provision.

11 Held in London in March 2007 and chaired by Stephen Bubb of the Association of Chief Executives of Voluntary Organisations.

The future role of the third sector in social and economic regeneration: final report   **57**

Box 4.3 Social Firms – a social enterprise approach to providing employment for disadvantaged groups

A Social Firm is a business set up specifically to create good quality jobs for people disadvantaged in the labour market. There are three core values that Social Firms will subscribe to within their businesses, which are orientated around enterprise, employment and empowerment. In this way example:

- at least 50 per cent of the firm's turnover is earned through sales of goods and/or services. (Lowest for Social Firms as at April 2005 was 66 per cent);

- more than 25 per cent of employees are people disadvantaged in the labour market;

- all employees have a contract of employment and market wage at or above national minimum wage; and, amongst other things; and,

- staff development is a priority for the firm to maximise each employee's ability and potential.

Pack-IT Product Promotions Limited was established in 1988 as a small enterprise carrying out light industrial packing services. It is now a thriving three-pronged business supplying mailing, storage and distribution and on-line fulfilment. It also provides specialised finishing services such as subscription fulfilment and cross matching of short-run hand mailings, full web-based real time stock control facilities and customer services capabilities.

Pack-IT was originally set up by Cardiff City Council to provide training opportunities and permanent paid employment for people with learning disabilities. However, the organisation is now independent. As a Social Firm and community business, Pack-IT employs 21 staff, half of whom have Down's Syndrome, are profoundly deaf or have behavioural and learning difficulties. Everyone at Pack-IT is paid above market rates and works full-time.

According to Social Firms UK, the national support agency for Social Firms, there are 137 businesses trading as Social Firms or emerging Social Firms. This has increased from 5 in 1996. The sector has created 1652 full time equivalent jobs, of which 859 (52 per cent) are held by disadvantaged people (primarily disadvantaged through disability).

www.socialfirms.co.uk

Opportunities in public service improvement

4.25 The Action Plan for Third Sector Public Service Delivery sets out a number of key areas where the third sector is able to contribute to public service transformation. Building on progress in all of these areas and the growing evidence base, the third sector review has identified four key opportunities for the 2007 CSR years, where the third sector, in partnership with Government can play an even greater role.

Transport   **4.26**   In transport, the third sector has a potential role in complementing existing provision particularly with regards to the Government's accessibility objectives. The review led by the Department for Transport in December, *Putting Passengers First*, identified that the third sector could potentially play a larger role in for example providing transport in rural areas, which would not be attractive to commercial operators, or even suitable for the traditional bus running to a fixed route and timetable.[12] The Office of the Third Sector will work alongside the Department for Transport (DfT) to ensure that the Local Transport Bill offers an opportunity for the Government to support greater third sector provision and delivery, by looking at eligibility rules which currently act as barriers.

Waste **4.27** The Department for Environment, Food and Rural Affairs (Defra) has been leading a review of waste strategy and have been clear that the Government should encourage third sector waste organisations in order to make the overall market more competitive, encourage innovation where there is no immediate commercial incentive and to facilitate the delivery of wider benefits. **The Waste and Resources Action Programme (WRAP) is therefore to develop a programme of work to grow the sector's capacity to help it compete to deliver waste and recycling services.**

Health and social care **4.28** The Department of Health's (DH) recent commissioning framework on health and wellbeing set out a requirement from 2008-09 for all Primary Care Trusts (PCTs) and Local Authorities to undertake a strategic needs assessment and consult with local communities on the package of services the community wants. The increased role for PCTs in commissioning and shaping services for local communities offers significant potential for the third sector – particularly where PCTs look for new ways to provide services that improve the quality and responsiveness of patient care. **Over the 2007 CSR years the Office of the Third Sector will work with DH to raise awareness of issues relating to third sector provision.**

Youth services **4.29** HM Treasury and the Department for Children, Schools and Families' (DCSF) 2007 CSR review on children and young people's policy has recognised the significant contribution made by the third sector to the delivery of positive activities. The ten year youth strategy will set out investment and reform to improve what's on offer to young people, including increasing the contribution of the third sector to delivering services in this area. In particular, recognising their skills in empowering young people and delivering packages of support and activities to very marginalised teenagers.

---

[12] Putting Passengers First, the Government's proposals for a modernised national framework for bus services, Department for Transport, December 2006.

Box 4.4 Housing Associations

The Government considers the housing association sector an integral part of the third sector. Since 1974, the housing association sector has grown rapidly through a mix of new development and large-scale stock transfer from local authorities and they are the fastest growing voluntary organisations in the country. Today, housing associations provide a home for around 5 million people across England.

Housing associations have led the way for their own improvement, through the iN business for neighbourhoods. Launched in 2003 by the National Housing Federation, iN business for neighbourhoods creates a charter for housing associations, made up of a set of commitments, such as being more customer and neighbourhood focussed, as well as creating a shared identity. Its aim is to help people identify that the same type of organisation is delivering a range of services in their neighbourhood.

Housing associations are well placed to assist in the development of participation strategies and community empowerment, to assist and facilitate third sector partnerships with private and public sectors or act as delivery agents for new social policy initiatives for example projects around financial inclusion. They are able to provide services to social enterprises such as payroll and HR advice and to raise collateral to resource projects using the strengths of their financial assets. Many housing associations also tackle financial inclusion as part of their rent arrears management; provide access to finance, lending institutions and commercial and business skills and provide employment and training opportunities or are involved in environmental sustainability initiatives.

The CHANGE partnership
Change is a partnership of 12 housing associations working in London and the South East. It aims to reduce financial exclusion amongst social housing residents. Set up initially by London and Quadrant Housing Trust, supported by Family Housing Association and Metropolitan Housing Trust in February 2003, Change is a registered Community Development Finance Institution.

Change has offered a variety of services and support to residents over the last 4 years, including working with the Department for Work and Pensions to support residents to make informed choices about having their welfare benefits & pensions paid direct into suitable accounts. In 2006/7 it trialled a personal lending scheme and is currently offering generic financial advice and banking support, alongside financial education for new and existing residents, as well as awareness training for frontline staff.

It also helps residents to access affordable credit services and to support them to take up products and services which are best suited to their needs. The biggest challenge ahead is to join with others in the third sector to develop programmes of scale that can be offered at economic cost across a wide customer group. Change is working with the National Housing Federation, Chartered Institute of Housing and others towards this wider objective.

4.30   Across public services, a small number of public services have been transferred into the third sector. This happened in the case of Leisure Trusts in the 1980s and is now being explored by DH through pathfinder projects looking at the significance of social enterprise models for PCTs. While transfers of this kind are likely to be appropriate in only a limited number of cases, they may offer opportunities to:

- roll out new services;

- embed particular spending priorities;

- enable new alliances; and,

- enable stronger community governance.

4.31 This option is most likely to be worth considering for organisations that are relatively small, networked with other organisations, community-focused, and experienced employers. They would also need to be operating within an environment of strong professional leadership in which commissioners are committed to innovation.

4.32 Organisations of this kind also face practical barriers to joining the third sector from the public sector, most significantly pensions. Work by the DH, HM Treasury and other Departments will contribute to the knowledge base about the areas in which transfers of this kind are possible and of benefit. However, Government is clear that any case for transferring public sector organisations into the third sector must demonstrate the benefits it will bring not only to individual organisations but to services to the public overall.

Demand-led funding **4.33** An important trend across systems of public services is the growth of models in which funding is allocated according to the decisions of individual citizens. For example, individual budgets are being used successfully within social care and the Learning and Skills Council is looking at the role demand-led funding can play within 14-19 education. Demand-led funding is potentially a very significant opportunity for third sector organisations, offering them the chance to grow their services where they are popular and effective.

4.34 However, demand-led funding may also bring some challenges for third sector organisations. The Action Plan for Third Sector Public Service Delivery established the principle that commissioners should ensure risk-sharing wherever appropriate in order to ensure efficiency and effectiveness. The need to share risk where appropriate remains important in the context of demand-led funding and public services will have to strike a careful balance between certainty and flexibility. **Over the next year, the Office of the Third Sector will engage in further work to understand the relationship between demand-led funding and funding for the third sector.**

Public Service Agreements **4.35** Public Service Agreements (PSAs) have played a vital role in galvanising public service delivery and achieving major improvements in outcomes since their introduction in the 1998 Comprehensive Spending Review. The 2007 CSR will build on the approach, driving ambitious improvements in priority areas while developing the supporting performance management framework to ensure a user-focused, devolved approach to public service delivery. The performance management framework in the 2007 CSR period will include:

- a comprehensive set of Strategic Objectives for each department;

- a focused set of PSAs which articulate the Government's highest priority outcomes for the spending period and will typically span several departments;

- a single cross-departmental Delivery Agreement for each PSA, developed in consultation with front line workers and users, supported by a basket of national, outcome focused indicators;

- an emphasis on central coordination working in synergy with greater bottom up accountability, local flexibility and user responsiveness; and,

- a premium on the use of high quality, timely data while freeing up the frontline by reducing low value data burdens.

4.36 The third sector's contribution to the delivery of PSAs will, where appropriate be embedded within Delivery Agreements, setting out actions to ensure high quality partnership with the third sector in the delivery chain, user engagement and the contribution of volunteering to the delivery of the outcome. Third sector experts have also been involved in the central peer review process that has been used in the development of PSAs.

Box 4.5 Action across Government in the 2007 CSR years

As part of CSR 2007, the Government will ensure that the third sector is embedded across the set of Public Services Agreements (PSAs): as a key partner in public service delivery; by ecognising the sector's role in engagement and advocacy for users; in the contribution of olunteers and through the overall delivery chain. Moreover:

The Department of Health will:

- publish a third sector strategy for the 2007 CSR period;

- take forward a Third Sector and Social Enterprise Delivery Board to oversee an integrated cross-cutting programme embedding the third sector as a key dimension in health and social care reform and delivery, while also taking forward the Commissioning Framework for Health and Wellbeing emphasising the need for person-centred, individual care and a key role for the third sector;

- produce a high-level Volunteering Strategy to build the profile of, and support for, volunteers and volunteering opportunities in the context of service reform in health and social care;

- carry out a strategic review which will look at funding of the third sector with the aim of reforming existing streams, including the S64 and Opportunities for Volunteering Schemes, into a more strategic portfolio of investment in the sector.

The Ministry of Justice will:

- ensure the third sector continues to play a key role in the delivery of legal aid over the 2007 CSR period and in the implementation of Community Legal Advice Centres and Networks, so that services can be tailored to the specific needs and priorities of local areas;

- continue its involvement with the third sector as a partner in supporting the work of Community Justice Centres, which aim to put the needs of the community at its core;

- build new ways of working with key bodies and local communities by: creating corporate stakeholder engagement, identifying relationships between stakeholder engagement and business performance, engaging Government Offices and creating a stakeholder database;

- use the Offender Management Bill to enable probation services to be commissioned from the best available provider, allowing services to be delivered by the public, third and private sector, often working in partnership together by playing to their strengths, with commissioners seeking to draw on the necessary contributions that other commissioners can make in respect of resources not managed by the Ministry of Justice;

- use the National Offender Management Service (NOMS) Commissioning Framework to provide the flexibility and freedom for Regional Offender Managers, the Director of Offender Management for Wales and regional and local delivery partners to innovate and deliver solutions to best meet local needs.

Action across Government in the 2007 CSR years

Communities and Local Government will:

- consult on a new third sector strategy (published June 2007);

- support communities and social enterprises by supporting community anchors to become self-sustaining through asset and enterprise development (as set out in Chapter 3);

- support voice and public services by reinforcing the need for partnership at the local level, enabling empowered communities to work with Local Government in place shaping (publishing draft 'place shaper' guidance and performance indicators in the autumn);

- support social enterprise by exploring a wider role for housing associations;

- minimise obstacles preventing good quality third sector providers from competing fairly to deliver housing support services through the Supporting People programme, ensuring that front-line third sector agencies receive appropriate development and support, with capacity building work to support smaller providers in particular;

- adopt a more coherent approach to direct engagement with the third sector through Strategic Partners, where three year funding would be the expectation, and a Third Sector Partnership Board (as set out in Chapter 2);

The Department for Children, Schools and Families will take forward the actions outlined in its third sector strategy for the 2007 CSR years (published in June 2007), including:

- raising the profile of volunteering and mentoring in schools;

- strengthening the focus on social enterprise as a career option and business model through the new curriculum framework and working with the QCA to build an understanding of social enterprise into accredited studies such as GCSE Business Studies and Diplomas

- opening up more markets, building in greater roles for non-statutory providers through legislation and guidance and ensuring that the ten year youth strategy takes advantage of third sector expertise;

- developing the skills of commissioners so that they can engage better with third sector providers;

- reviewing regional commissioning models to ensure they promote diversity of provision, reflecting both the nature of different providers and the size of different organisations.

The Department for Environment, Food and Rural Affairs will:

- explore opportunities to use the CSR07 process to improve the way it purchases public value from the third sector — specifically through better funding arrangements and mitigating the risks associated with any changes to programmes and priorities;

- ensure that implementation of the newly published Waste Strategy reflects aspirations for the third sector to play a greater role in delivering objectives and quality outcomes in this area, and make full use of the third sector to tackle climate change.

Action across Government in the 2007 CSR years

The Department for Work and Pensions will:

- by 2008, implement Pathways to Work in those areas of the country that do not currently have Pathways coverage. This will create a significant opportunity for the third sector to bid to deliver Pathways support, either as individual bidders or as part of consortia. The roll-out will take place in phases.

The Department for Business, Enterprise and Regulatory Reform will:

- ensure that proposals for future business support, delivered through Business Link reflects the needs and priorities of organisations, groups and people working in social enterprises as well as other types of business;

- improve the information and guidance available to social enterprise on the businesslink.gov website;

- with the National Council for Graduate Entrepreneurship, run a series of workshops promoting social enterprise start-ups in the English Universities, as part of the Flying Start Rallies;

- develop a third sector strategy and action plan.

The Department for Innovation, Universities and Skills will:

- work in consultation with the Sector Skills Development Agency and other partners to develop a programme of action to address skills issues for the sector;

- continue progress in enabling access by volunteers to Train to Gain.

The Government Olympic Executive at the Department for Culture, Media and Sport will:

- work with partners to encourage active participation by people across the country in sport, culture, and in communities, inspired by hosting the 2012 Olympic and Paralympic Games. 70,000 volunteers will be engaged for the Games - the largest volunteer force in peace time Britain - already over 140,000 people have registered an interest;

- take forward the Pre-volunteering programme (PVP) being piloted in London. This targets unemployed people from hard to reach groups, using the hook of the 2012 Games, to develop skills, which will prepare people for work. The training will include volunteering and all graduates will be offered an interview for volunteering at the Games;

- work with the Department for Business, Enterprise and regulatory Reform and engage with the third sector to ensure local communities are involved in the development of the Games and that local enterprises can engage with business opportunities.

Building capacity

4.37   The Government invests in the capacity of third sector organisations to deliver public services through for example the Futurebuilders Fund and the investments being made by the Department of Health in social enterprise solutions in health and social care. The DH has committed £73 million over the 2007 CSR years to promote social enterprise delivery and has already invested in 26 pathfinder projects.

Futurebuilders   **4.38**   A report from the Futurebuilders Advisory Panel in 2006 highlighted the innovative nature of the Futurebuilders Fund that has been driving increasingly high quality applications for loan and grant finance and is gaining momentum in terms of investments made. Since it was launched, Futurebuilders has made 239 investments totalling £101.9 million to 225 schemes. Futurebuilders are providing a range of innovative tailored investment packages and are receiving positive feedback from the third sector organisations they interact with, enabling them to deliver more public services. An interim report of the evaluation of Futurebuilders, carried out by Sheffield Hallam University, will be completed in the summer. The report will examine the working arrangements of Futurebuilders, its effect on organisational development in the third sector and its impact on service users. A final formal evaluation report will be presented in October 2010.

4.39   In April 2007, the Government announced that as the first phase of the Futurebuilders programme comes to an end, the Cabinet Office will tender a new contract to deliver the Fund from 2008 to 2011 demonstrating the continued commitment to building third sector capacity to transform public services. Over the 2007 CSR, the Government will commit up to £65 million for the Futurebuilders Fund, bringing the total investment in the programme to £215 million by 2011, as set out in the 2004 spending review.

4.40   Responding to the recommendation in the report of the Futurebuilders Advisory Panel, Budget 2007 also announced that when the contract is re-let, the Fund will be open to all third sector organisations, operating in a broader range of areas of public service delivery. Through the tendering process, the Government will also explore with potential providers the scope for the provision of more innovative forms of finance.

> **Box 4.6 Waveney Crossroads Ltd: Futurebuilders 200th investee**
>
> Waveney Crossroads is the main provider of respite care for carers in the Waveney district of Suffolk. It offers traditional 'in the home' care services and day services from two centres in Lowestoft. Waveney recently secured a new building to increase the number of days it can offer to adults and introduced new family support services including a weekend club for children with disabilities and a carers group.
>
> The £157,500 Futurebuilders investment is supporting Waveney expand its provision through a £97,500 loan to refurbish and equip the new centre and a £60,000 revenue grant to fund the establishment of a new Development Manager for two years to identify and diversify new income streams.
>
> An increase in day care provision provides significant benefits to carers and the people they care for. Waveney has been proactive in seeking different ways to expand their services to ensure they meet the needs of the local area and local authority. As well as continuing to deliver traditional respite care services, the new centre will bring distinctive benefits to carers in the form of family support services and access to relevant health and social care organisations.

Innovation and learning from the sector

4.41   Effective public services depend on successful innovation through developing better ways of meeting needs, solving problems and using resources and technologies in order to increase efficiency and improve experiences and outcomes for citizens. The Government recognises the concern within the third sector that too often insights that could transform people's lives are lost because innovators struggle to find the advice, support and contacts they need to advance and grow their ideas. Following a competition launched by the Government in March 2006, the Innovation Unit, working with ACEVO and others, will create an Innovation Exchange, bringing together third sector innovators and commissioners of public services to develop and spread the most innovative practice. The Exchange will use £1.2 million over three years to pilot new approaches to finding innovators within the third sector the resources and support they need to develop and grow their work.

Box 4.7 Learning from the Invest to Save Budget

The Invest to Save Budget (ISB) is a grant-funding programme aimed at promoting partnership, efficiency and innovation. The fund was re-branded following the 2004 Spending Review, with a focus on the third sector's role in delivering public services within local communities. This follows growing recognition of the sector's role in delivering local services, particularly in designing innovative approaches to engaging with deprived and hard to reach communities. Since 2004, the total investment in the third sector stands at over £100 million.

The ISB third sector portfolio provides useful evidence and learning on the value of third sector innovation to public service delivery, whether a grant funding stream has been successful in supporting it, as well as some of the barriers to sustaining it in the long term.

Key areas of third sector innovation supported by the ISB include in health and social care services, children and family services, employment and skills and information and advice.

Innovative approaches include:

- flexible and holistic service delivery;

- complementing or enhancing the 'standard' approach;

- taking preventative approaches to social problems with the aim of reducing the pressures and costs of recourse to statutory services; and

- facilitating access to services for particular groups and communities through the provision of independent advice, mentoring and advocacy support.

Key successes and remaining barriers

One of the most notable outcomes of ISB has been the opportunity it has provided to third sector organisations and their services to get involved at a strategic level and to influence policy development and service design. Learning from successful and unsuccessful ISB projects has influenced the development of local strategies as well as national policy.

A key barrier to sustaining innovative services is access to continuation funding. Successful projects have implemented robust sustainability strategies from the outset and incorporated a system of ongoing evaluation throughout the life of the project to ensure that the early benefits and achievements can be promoted.

The rolling out and embedding of successful innovative approaches on a larger, sustainable scale cannot be achieved without the longer-term commitment of resources and investment from government. Successful projects have benefited from the commitment of senior policy leads within central and local government.

Effective risk management is imperative to supporting innovation in public services. The ISB, because of its focus on partnership, encourages risk management to be jointly owned and managed. Good communication mechanisms and effective joint working across organisations at both the strategic and operational levels have encouraged effective risk management.

www.isb.gov.uk

5

ENCOURAGING SOCIAL ENTERPRISE

Summary

The Government recognises the potential of businesses that want to combine profit generation with social and environmental goals.

The Government will:

- invest further in raising awareness of the social enterprise business model so that new audiences are aware of the potential of the choices they can make in setting up a business or buying from one;

- ensure that young people know about social enterprise, through their enterprise and business studies education. Social enterprise will be part of the main key stage 3 and 4 curriculum framework from 2008, and the Qualifications and Curriculum Authority is currently consulting on how best to include social enterprise models in the GCSE Business Studies syllabus;

- through the third sector research programme, invest in building the evidence about the impact and nature of the social enterprise sector;

- work to improve the business support that is available for people wanting to start and grow social enterprises, through Business Link and capacity building support from Capacitybuilders;

- work to improve social enterprises access to finance including through delivery of the £10 million equity fund announced in the Social Enterprise Action Plan and by examining ways to boost social investment; and,

- support Government Departments to investigate how social enterprise business models can improve policy delivery and outcomes.

INTRODUCTION

5.1   The Social Enterprise Action Plan, published in November 2006, sets out a vision for dynamic social enterprises contributing to a stronger economy and fairer society with actions to begin to create the conditions for thousands more social enterprises.[1] There are at least 55,000 social enterprises, with a combined turnover of £27 billion and a contribution to GDP estimated to be around £8.4 billion.[2] As businesses, but part of the third sector, social enterprises engage in trading or contracting to create surpluses to reinvest either within the business or in its wider social or environmental mission.[3] The social enterprise sector operates in the full range of activities in the economy and encompasses a wide diversity of organisations including businesses trading entirely in commercial markets and those delivering key public services on behalf of Government.

---

[1] Social enterprise action plan, Scaling new heights, Cabinet Office, November 2006.

[2] Annual Small Business Survey, Department for Trade and Industry, 2005.

[3] The Government definition of a social enterprise is a 'business with primarily social objectives whose surpluses are principally reinvested for that purpose in the business or in the community, rather than being driven by the need to maximise profit for shareholders and owners.'

Social enterprises all however, offer a new way of doing business, with the business model driven by the social and environmental mission.

5.2   The combination of producing social, economic and/or environmental returns, through a business approach contributes to multiple Government objectives around meeting social and environmental needs, increasing enterprise, improving public services and promoting ethical markets. In this way, the Government recognises the contribution of social enterprise across the variety of roles the third sector plays, in building communities, promoting voice and in the delivery and design of public services. There is also benefit in Government promoting enterprising solutions within the wider third sector, supporting organisations to achieve sustainability, through diversification of income streams and development of trading strategies, where appropriate.

THE CONSULTATION

5.3   The interim report of the third sector review highlighted that the consultation responses on promoting enterprising solutions within the third sector had focused on issues such as:

- the concept of social enterprise needs a higher profile, with a lack of understanding about the business model itself and its potentially additional impact relative to other ways of tackling social and environmental need. The impact of this lack of understanding can be felt in several arenas, including when social enterprises are looking for commercial finance, when seeking public sector delivery contracts and in explaining the message to consumers;

- there is no mechanism for sharing the best practice and learning within the sector, many organisations felt they were delivering innovative solutions to local problems but that this learning cannot be shared more widely;

- where provision of business support to social enterprise is good, the benefits are keenly felt, however respondents to the consultation said that provision through the Government's main channel – Business Link was uneven and sometimes difficult to navigate;

- access to finance is a clear issue for social enterprises although the financing picture appears to be getting better – particularly with regard to debt finance. There are issues around the ability and confidence of smaller social enterprises to gain finance and at the larger end of the scale in terms of accessing risk capital;

- the social enterprise sector alongside other third sector organisations report difficulties in accessing contacts to deliver public services as set out in Chapter 4.

> ### Box 5.1 The Social Enterprise Action Plan: Scaling new heights
>
> The Social Enterprise Action Plan sets out measures in four key areas to respond to the concerns highlighted in the third sector review consultation:
>
> **Fostering a culture of social enterprise** – the Government has appointed a consortium led by the Social Enterprise Coalition to deliver a new programme to recruit and support at least 20 social enterprise ambassadors to raise awareness of social enterprise. It also continues to support the Make Your Mark: Change Lives campaign led by Enterprise Insight to promote social enterprise to young people. The Government will promote social enterprise within the curriculum and develop a new research programme to build further the evidence on the economic, social and environmental impact of the sector.
>
> **Ensuring the right information and advice is available to those running social enterprises** – the Government is providing additional funding to Regional Development Agencies to improve Business Link's capacity to broker business support for social enterprise. The Government is also improving the social enterprise information and guidance on the Business Link website.
>
> **Enabling social enterprises to access appropriate finance** – following consultation with the sector to determine a suitable model of delivery, the Government will make £10 million available for equity investment in social enterprise and will roll out financial awareness training for social enterprises.
>
> **Enabling social enterprises to work with Government** – including through the measures set out in the Action Plan for Third Sector Public Service Delivery and highlighting work across departments to increase public service delivery by social enterprise in health, waste management and in the delivery of the Olympics. The Government is also providing additional support to organisations representing social enterprises to ensure the voice of social enterprises are heard, to enable the sector to raise its own profile, and to influence public policy

THE FUTURE ROLE OF THE THIRD SECTOR IN ENCOURAGING SOCIAL ENTERPRISE

5.4   An enterprising approach to delivering social change will be achieved through the vision that:

- social enterprises themselves are able to grow and thrive and that the conditions are created for the development of thousands more businesses; and,

- all organisations in the third sector have access to appropriate forms of support so that they can diversify their income streams, including through trading, if they choose to take this route.

5.5   Feedback from the social enterprise thematic roundtable held as part of the review suggests that the social enterprise sector is determined that it can grow in all areas of the economy and that the wider economy increasingly recognises the social and environmental value, social enterprises can produce.[4] In the future, the attendees at the roundtable believe that consumers and commissioners should always have a clear and informed choice that includes a social enterprise option. This will require a

---

[4] Held in Bristol, in February 2007 and chaired by Jonathan Bland of the Social Enterprise Coalition.

harnessing of the marketing power of the sector, so consumers, along with the public and private sectors are aware of the choices that can be made. The social enterprise sector itself has a clear role in raising awareness of the impact that social enterprise models can make. Social enterprises themselves must not shy away from attaining the business skills and discipline required for growth, for promotion of the sector and for measuring and communicating their impact.

5.6   Alongside this, the Government has a role in creating the conditions primarily in the business support and finance markets to enable social enterprises and other third sector organisations to grow. The Government's role in promoting social enterprise is to identify and provide support to overcome market failures that present barriers to growth. In many instances, this market failure may be an asymmetry in the information available to either consumers or those in the public or private sector who might support enterprise growth, either by providing finance or by contracting for business.

5.7   Government believes that overcoming the barriers to social enterprise growth will result in progress in tackling some of society's most entrenched social and environmental challenges; setting new standards for ethical markets and corporate responsibility; improving public services; and attracting new people into business and the third sector. Moreover, this progress will be facilitated by and will itself drive increasing societal trends in which people are making increasingly ethical decisions about what they want to purchase and where they want to work.

Box 5.2 The rising tide of ethical consumerism

According to The Ethical Consumerism Report 2006 published by the Co-operative Bank, the value of UK ethical consumerism grew to £29.3 billion in 2005, up 11 per cent on the previous year and valued higher than the retail market for tobacco and alcohol for the first time. The total covers spending on ethical food including organic and Fairtrade products; green home expenditure; eco-travel and transport costs; humane cosmetics and eco-fashion; and ethical finance and investments. Of this, consumer spend specifically to address climate change totalled £3.8 million.

Moreover, more people than ever reported that they recycled (94 per cent), supported local shops and suppliers (80 per cent), avoided a product or service on the basis of a company's reputation (55 per cent), or actively chose a product or service on the basis of a company's responsible reputation (61 per cent).

5.8   The Social Enterprise Action Plan set out a strategy that the Government is committed to implement through the 2007 CSR years, with funding allocations made for example on business support through the Regional Development Agencies and for the social enterprise strategic partners up to 2011. In addition the Government recognises that more can be done to promote the value of social enterprise, to understand the particular business needs of social enterprise and to embed the concept of social enterprise in wider Government policy development, whether that be through third sector interventions or in wider public policy delivery.

Fostering a culture of social enterprise

5.9   The Social Enterprise Action plan highlighted that only around 26 per cent of people were familiar with the concept of social enterprise.[5] This lack of knowledge may have several important knock-on effects including that individuals do not know about the possibilities of a business approach to tackling social and environmental challenges, and as discussed above consumers, whether individuals or organisations in the public and private sectors may be unaware of the choices that can be made in purchasing and contracting. The Government has a role in building awareness, and in empowering the social enterprise sector to promote the role of social enterprise based on a solid body of evidence.

5.10   Social enterprise is part of wider Government efforts to encourage an enterprising culture. Overall attitudes towards entrepreneurship are improving, with the proportion of young people aged 16-24 considering going into business having risen from 14 per cent in 2003 to 18 per cent in 2005.[6] There have also been increases in the number of people who encourage friends to start their own business and a decline in adverse attitudes to starting businesses, over the same timeframe.

Make Your Mark campaign   **5.11**   The Make Your Mark campaign, run by Enterprise Insight and funded by the Department of Business, Enterprise and Regulatory Reform, aims to help create a more enterprising culture amongst young people in the UK. A major part of the campaign is an annual Enterprise Week. Since starting in 2004, Enterprise Week has involved over 6,000 events with attendance of over 1 million and more than £10 million worth of media coverage. Make Your Mark focuses mainly on people in their teens and twenties, helping them to develop enterprising ideas and attitudes as they transition from education to adult life. A new element of the campaign, Make Your Mark: Change Lives, embeds promotion of social enterprise within the wider campaign. The Government is working with a wide partnership of organisations, all interested in encouraging enterprising young people to use their ideas for social and environmental change, to maximise the impact of the "Change Lives" campaign.

Social enterprise Ambassadors   **5.12**   The Social Enterprise Action Plan included a new social enterprise Ambassadors programme. The Ambassadors will raise awareness of social enterprise and aim to attract new people to the sector. They are likely to be established social entrepreneurs who can be dynamic advocates for the kind of social and environmental change that social enterprise can achieve. They will target a range of audiences from the classroom to the boardroom. Following consultation with the sector about the shape of the programme, a consortium led by the Social Enterprise Coalition won the contract to develop and deliver a high impact programme to find, nurture and promote these high profile role models. Recruitment of Ambassadors will be open and transparent, and the Ambassadors will be in place to take part in Social Enterprise Day on 15 November 2007.

5.13   In June 2007, the Government announced new funding for seven social enterprise strategic partners able to represent the voice of the social enterprise sector. Part of the funding will be used by each partner to promote social enterprise and to contribute to the Make Your Mark Campaign. However, there is more that can be done, both in scope and scale, to target new audience segments and to produce the materials to support this awareness raising effort.

---

[5] Household Survey, Small Business Service, DTI, 2006.

[6] Household Survey of Entrepreneurship, DTI 2005.

Promotion of social enterprise

5.14 Over the 2007 CSR years, the Government will commit further funding to promotional activity around attracting new entrants, and complementary work to engage intermediaries and potential customers. The Government will seek to consult a range of stakeholders on the programme (as set out in Chapter 2) and establish a steering group, to identify the gaps in current activity and advise on ways to reach new audiences, making sure the various strands of activity on establishing a social enterprise culture are complementary where appropriate. Further details on funding and the design of the consultation will be available later in the year.

5.15 The Government will consult with the social enterprise sector to develop ideas on priorities that will complement the existing Ambassadors programme, strategic funding and Make Your Mark: Change Lives. New work could include developing an understanding of the motivations of potential new entrants to social enterprise from other backgrounds – for example business people seeking a career change, diverse groups, and those with expertise in potential growth areas for social enterprise. It could include creation of promotional or guidance material, events and visits, or improvement to existing sources of information. Government will also support work to improve knowledge of social enterprise to secondary audiences such as intermediaries (e.g. the professions) and potential customers in the public and private sector.

Raising awareness through the education system

5.16 Within the education system, enterprise capability is defined as "creativity, innovation, risk-management and risk-taking, and a can-do attitude and the drive to make ideas happen"; and enterprise education as "enterprise capability, supported by better financial capability and economic and business understanding". The Government is committed to strengthening further the UK's enterprise culture and is working to promote even greater enterprise capability among young people in education. As set out in Budget 2007, over the 2007 CSR years, this work will continue with continued funding for enterprise education in schools of £180 million.

5.17 The Government has recognised that in order to build a society in which people have full information about the possibilities of the social enterprise business model, learning about social enterprise must be embedded in the education system. Social enterprise models and examples offer pupils and teachers an attractive and accessible means of underpinning the objectives of enterprise education. Social enterprise will become part of the main key stage 3 and 4 curriculum framework from 2008, and the Qualifications and Curriculum Authority is currently consulting on how best to include social enterprise models in the GCSE Business Studies syllabus.

Building the evidence

5.18 There is a growing evidence base on the contribution of social enterprise to a range of social, economic and environmental outcomes and through the Annual Small Business Survey, a baseline of the numbers of social enterprise and their contribution as part of the small business population. However, analysis for the Social Enterprise Coalition has suggested that there continue to be evidence gaps, reflecting the relative newness of the field in research terms.[7] These areas include understanding the dynamics of social enterprises, the contribution of social enterprise to economic productivity, the social and environmental impacts of social enterprises, the contribution of the sector to public service delivery and reform and around the rise of ethical consumerism. There is also a clear need to understand better the financing needs of social enterprise models, particularly around the desire for equity based funding. What is key will be to generate a greater understanding around what is unique

---

[7] Referenced by permission from the Social Enterprise Coalition.

about social enterprise models relative to other means of delivering social and economic outcomes.

5.19 The Social Enterprise Action Plan committed to a new research programme to build further the evidence on the economic, social and environmental value of the sector and on ethical consumer markets. Part of this research programme is a series of think pieces commissioned by Government, which will be short, sharp papers exploring issues around social enterprise and innovation, ethical markets, employment and measuring value.

5.20 The Government believes that building the social enterprise evidence base is a priority for the 2007 CSR years. Chapter 6 sets out details of a new programme to build evidence across the third sector, backed by new investment from Government and the research community. Social enterprise will be one of the key workstreams of this programme.

Box 5.3 Divine Chocolate

In autumn 1998, Divine, the first ever Fairtrade chocolate bar aimed at the mass market was launched in the UK. In an exciting new business model, the co-operative of cocoa farmers in Ghana (Kuapa KoKoo) own a significant share of the company. This is critical for Divine as being farmer-owned means that the farmers not only participate in decision-making, but also in profits as suppliers and owners. In 2006 the company paid its first dividends to shareholders, with turnover at almost £9 million.

Divine Chocolate Limited is a social enterprise formed as a private company limited by shares. From the outset its 99 ordinary shares were owned by three parties; 52 per cent by the Fairtrade NGO Twin Trading, 33 per cent owned by Kuapa Kokoo farmers co-operative and 14 per cent owned by the international retailer Body Shop International. At the time of start up the Department for International Development provided a loan guarantee enabling the company to borrow funds to get started.

In July 2006 The Body Shop made the decision to donate its shares in Divine Chocolate to Kuapa Kokoo, giving the cooperative a greater stake in the business.

The overall strategic aim of Divine Chocolate is to improve the livelihood of smallholder cocoa producers in West Africa by establishing their own dynamic branded proposition in the UK chocolate market, thus putting them higher up the value chain. To achieve this mission a range of clear intermediate objectives are set out:

- to take a quality and affordable range of Fairtrade chocolate into the UK mainstream market.

- to pay a Fairtrade price for all the cocoa used in the chocolate sold.

- to raise awareness of fair trade issues among UK retailers and consumers of all age groups.

- to be highly visible and vocal in the chocolate sector and thereby act as a catalyst for change.

On February 14th 2007 the launch of Divine Chocolate Inc in the USA was announced.

Ensuring the right information and advice is available to those running social enterprises

5.21   The *review of sub-national economic development and regeneration* published in July 2007 sets out reforms to refocus powers and responsibilities to ensure economic prosperity for all.[8] This includes giving a greater role for Local Authorities in ensuring economic opportunity for all, with strengthened powers and incentives to support prosperity, and clearer regional strategies where Regional Development Agencies (RDAs) are expected to develop a single integrated regional strategy which sets out the economic, social and environmental objectives for each region. In developing regional strategies, RDAs will consult widely with businesses, Local Authorities, trade unions, the education sector, third sector groups and others. The RDAs will continue to play a key role in coordinating business support within the regions, through the integrated regional strategies and in delivery, through the Business Link channel.

Business support   **5.22**   The Government wants to promote the conditions in which business can prosper and can benefit from accessing appropriate business support. In many instances, social enterprises require similar advice and support to mainstream businesses. The Government has a role in ensuring that businesses are able to find the most appropriate support available to them in the market, and does so through the Business Link gateway, managed by the RDAs. Business Link provides information, and if appropriate diagnoses of individual needs and brokers support from the appropriate specialist providers.

5.23   As part of the plans to reduce the number of business support services offered from over 3,000 to 100 or fewer by 2010, providing overall a more streamlined and easily accessible route to business support, the Business Link brand and channel for business support will be strengthened over the 2007 CSR years. In June 2007, the Government issued a consultation document seeking views from business and other stakeholders on the proposals for the design of the new portfolio of Government business support.[9] The consultation seeks views on the business support Government might fund in the future, reflecting what business says it needs and where Government has identified a need to intervene, how Business Link can be developed as the primary access point to signpost businesses to get advice and support and how to avoid the future proliferation of business support schemes. Social enterprises are encouraged to respond to the consultation, which will inform Government decisions on business support in the 2007 CSR years. The consultation closes on the 14th September 2007.

5.24   The Government's aim for social enterprise is that they are able to maximise their performance and impact, and access the appropriate support to enable them to do that. Over the next ten years, the Government is aiming to encourage the development of a sustainable market for social enterprise support, where social enterprises access support on a similar basis to other businesses. In this way, the Government wants to encourage more social enterprises to use the support available to them through the Business Link gateway.

---

[8] Review of sub-national economic development and regeneration, HM Treasury, July 2007.

[9] Simplifying business support: a consultation, Department of Trade and Industry, June 2007.

5.25   Research undertaken by Rocket Science[10] and by the Social Enterprise Coalition has suggested that there are some key issues that affect the availability of support that can lead to social enterprises improving their performance.[11]   These include social enterprises being able and willing to access support, having support that is focused on the needs of the customer, mainstream and specialist support organisations working in partnership, having quality assured support organisations and advisers and understanding the scale of social enterprise activity and the scale of support required in a particular area. As set out in the Social Enterprise Action Plan and subsequent social enterprise business support guidance for RDAs, these factors for success are forming the basis for additional funding to the RDAs to improve Business Link's capacity to broker business support for social enterprise.[12] The funding will look to address the market failures present in business support provision for social enterprise. This includes that social enterprise are not accessing business support as much as they could, the lack of understanding within Business Link of the needs of social enterprise, the inability or unwillingness of social enterprises to purchase high quality support, and the lack of capacity in social enterprise support agencies. **Through the 2007 CSR years, the additional funding for RDAs is confirmed at £1.8 million each year.**

Capacitybuilders   **5.26**   It is also critical that business support provision is coordinated with the infrastructure in place at a local and regional level to support other third sector organisations. Local infrastructure organisations should be able to provide advice and information to organisations seeking to diversify income streams and reach sustainability, and should be able to point organisations towards sources of appropriate business support. At a local level, this will require additional joint working and understanding between third sector infrastructure and mainstream business support provision. **Capacitybuilders will work with the RDAs and other appropriate agencies to build the capacity of social enterprise infrastructure organisations, particularly where there are clear market failures. Capacitybuilders will report on social enterprise support in its annual evaluation.**

5.27   Chapter 6 sets out details of work to develop and implement a skills strategy for the third sector. This skills strategy will include the development of skills needed for the social enterprise sector.

---

[10] Mapping regional approaches to business support for social enterprise, Cabinet Office 2007

[11] Policy paper on business support, Social Enterprise Coalition, 2006.

[12] Social enterprise business support. Guidance for Regional Development Agencies, Cabinet Office, 2007.

Box 5.4 Community Interest Companies

The Government launched the Community Interest Company (CIC) in 2005, providing a lightly regulated legal form for social enterprise. The first new legal form of company for 100 years.

CICs are limited companies with special additional features for people who want to create businesses that pursue a double or triple bottom line - profits alongside social and/or environmental change, but without the regulatory regime associated with having charitable status. CICs have the same tax treatment and legal structure as companies however to ensure that they use their assets and profits for the community interest:

- they have an asset lock restricting profit and asset distribution. The ability to take assets out of the CIC in the form of dividends is subject to a cap of base rate +5 per cent, up to a maximum of 35 per cent of distributable income in a given year. Assets of wound up companies can only be passed to other asset locked bodies; and,

- they must pass a community interest test - whether a reasonable person could consider their activities to benefit the community – and produce an annual community interest report.

On 6 April 2007 further legislation came into force making it possible to form, or to convert to, a community interest company in Northern Ireland and making the CIC Regulator's office the Regulator of Community Interest Companies for the UK. In addition to the Regulator's main duties of processing applications, investigating complaints and where necessary taking enforcement action, the Regulator is responsible for raising awareness of CICs among those who advise and fund them. This outreach work has resulted in a steady increase in the number of applications

The 1,000th CIC was established in June 2007 - City Healthcare Partnership CIC will provide all primary and community health services across the City of Hull and is being established by the staff of Hull PCT Directly Managed Provider Unit.

The CIC regulator's 2006-07 annual report suggests that key areas of activity for CICs are in social and personal services, housing, education and health and social work.

Enabling social enterprise to access appropriate funding

5.28   Social enterprises, like all businesses have a range of finance needs and seek finance from a large variety of different sources in the public and private sector. The Government wants to ensure that viable social enterprises are able to access the finance they need and will make interventions in the market for finance, where there is evidence of market failure. Evidence from a recent survey of the financing needs of social enterprises and other small and medium sized enterprises (SMEs) has been examined to establish a picture on the demand for finance.[13] This research highlights that the percentage of social enterprises using commercial finance (65.5 per cent) is lower than the figure amongst for profit enterprises (79.8 per cent) and that the difference is more acute for smaller businesses.

---

[13] Finance for Small and Medium Sized Enterprises: Comparisons of Social Enterprises and Mainstream Businesses, 2007.

5.29 Some of the evidence suggests that part of the difference is due to social enterprises not applying for finance or limiting the scale of their demand:

- looking at size-bands, social enterprises with 1-9 employees are more likely to feel discouraged than their mainstream counterparts to seek commercial finance; and

- social enterprises in the 10-49 size-band received on average around three times less than the amount received on average by mainstream businesses. A similar finding holds amongst businesses in the 50-249 size-band, with social enterprises receiving almost 18 times less than mainstream enterprises. However, in both cases the proportions obtained relative to the amount sought were similar for both SMEs and social enterprises.

5.30 Other evidence suggests that existing demand is not being met:

- upon being rejected commercial finance, more mainstream enterprises are able to obtain funding from elsewhere than social enterprises; and,

- a greater percentage of social enterprises than mainstream enterprises have to defer their plans following rejection of commercial funding.

5.31 Possible reasons for these findings suggested by the survey include insufficient security and it could be that lenders are looking for more reassurance on what they perceive to be riskier deals, either due to a correct analysis of risk or due to a lack of familiarity with this sector. Some lenders have in the past cited moral hazard as an additional barrier to lending to this sector (i.e. they suffer reputational damage if a social enterprise that they have lent to fails), which may make them even more risk averse. Industry risk is cited by 17.9 per cent of social enterprises and 2.3 per cent of mainstream enterprises. This may relate to a lack of understanding by lenders of the legal and governance structures of social enterprises and of the business environment in which they are operating.

Community Development Finance   **5.32** This lack of awareness in the mainstream finance sector is one of the reasons why Community Development Finance Institutions (CDFIs) play an important role in lending to social enterprises, proving to commercial lenders that these are viable deals. Around 14 per cent of CDFIs concentrate on lending to social enterprises, with 69 per cent overall currently serving social enterprise (expected to rise to around 71 per cent). Over 50 per cent of lending by value is to social enterprise, which in 2005 amounted to over £27 million.[14] Budget 2007 announced that to ensure sustainability of the Community Development Finance sector, the Government will liaise with the banking sector, including the European Investment Bank and CDFIs, to explore how the framework for supporting the sector could be developed further.

Futurebuilders   **5.33** As set out in Chapter 4, the Futurebuilders fund provides grant and loan finance to third sector organisations looking to build capacity for the delivery of public services. In the 2007 CSR years, Futurebuilders will be opened up to investments across public service delivery. As set out by the independent Futurebuilders Advisory Panel, the Futurebuilders fund is delivering an innovative funding model for the sector, however the re-contracting process will also drive further innovation in funding practices for the Futurebuilders fund. The Government will be encouraging organisations to come forward with proposals for delivering through Futurebuilders, different financing options for organisations, which may include the existing package of development

---

[14] Inside Out. The state of Community Development Finance, CDFA, 2005.

grants and loans, but also quasi-equity type investments, which may be particularly relevant for the social enterprise sector.

Asset development   **5.34**   Many social enterprises such as Development Trusts are able to work towards sustainability through the generation of income via their asset base. The consultation, along with analysis undertaken for the Quirk Review, has highlighted the importance of a sustainable asset base for the sector and the Government will commit to supporting this through continued funding for community anchors, and ensuring ongoing progress on the Community Assets Fund. Communities and Local Government will also take forward the recommendations of the Quirk review as set out in Chapter 3.

Raising equity finance   **5.35**   A further issue is that many social enterprises choose structures which limit their ability to raise equity finance, or to provide a market return on investment. A report by the Bank of England into the financing of social enterprises in 2003 highlighted the frequently lower financial return, the lack of clear exit routes and the lack of a secondary market in inhibiting the supply of equity to social enterprises. On the demand side, some social enterprises (as other small businesses) are reluctant to give up control of the business to external investors who might influence the mission of the organisation, and this in turn may limit demand.[15]

5.36   However, there are investors willing to take a blended social and financial return, if the structures are clear, and there is some incentive for them to do so. Café Direct is one example of a social enterprise that has successfully raised share capital. Budget 2007 announced that the Office of the Third Sector would consider the evidence around levels of equity investment in social enterprises and whether they are lower than other SMEs due to market imperfections in the supply or whether it is due to traditional forms of equity not being appropriate for social enterprises

5.37   To address this specific issue around equity finance for social enterprise, the Social Enterprise Action Plan announced £10 million to be made available for co-investment with the private sector in social enterprises. **The Office of the Third Sector has been working to devise a structure for the fund and will to go out to consultation over the summer.**

Social stock exchange   **5.38**   To address the reported barrier of the lack of a secondary market for investments in social enterprises, the Office of the Third Sector is supporting research into the feasibility of a "social" capital market in which investors interested in a blended social and financial return might be able to make and trade investments. The Office is currently talking to the social enterprise and financial sectors to determine the appetite for establishing a social stock exchange.

Unclaimed assets and social investment   **5.39**   The 2005 Pre-Budget Report (PBR) announced the commitment of the Government and the bank and building society sector to develop a scheme to access genuinely unclaimed assets lying dormant in accounts and reinvest them to the benefit of society, whilst retaining a right for customers to reclaim their assets at any time. [16]

5.40 The Government published a consultation document in May 2007 setting out proposals for the most effective means of distributing unclaimed assets to the benefit of communities.[17] The document outlined the issues, which the Government believes should be the primary focus for the use of unclaimed assets in England, namely youth

---

15 The Financing of Social Enterprises, Bank of England, 2003.

16 Pre-Budget Report, Britain meeting the global challenge: Enterprise, fairness and responsibility, HM Treasury, December 2005.

17 Unclaimed assets distribution mechanism: a consultation, HM Treasury, Office of the Third Sector, May 2007.

services followed by financial capability and inclusion. Resources permitting, the Government would also like to see a proportion of the available assets in England used to invest in the long-term sustainability of the third sector and boost the social investment market; that is, investment made for a social purpose in organisations that are committed to delivering benefits for society and the environment.

5.41 The independent Commission for Unclaimed Assets, and other commentators, believe that the social investment market is underdeveloped, which, in turn, undermines the potential of the third sector itself to deliver social change.[18] The Commission has proposed the introduction of a wholesale institution – a Social Investment Bank - to build the capacity of financial intermediaries and to attract new, private capital to the third sector. In the mainstream finance markets this role is played by investment banks. Investment banks operate across the globe, financing the trading and commercial activities of other organisations, through, for example, corporate finance and advisory work, investment management and securities trading.

5.42 Applying this model to the social investment market would result in an organisation that would act as a wholesale distributor of funds to existing and new finance providers, carrying out activities such as:

- capitalising the organisations that invest in and lend to the third sector to enable them to meet the demand for their services;

- attracting capital investment to the sector;

- providing guarantees;

- promoting and trading in a secondary market for securities; and,

- encouraging the use of financial advice and business support by third sector organisations and intermediaries.

5.43 This function could be fulfilled by a new organisation or by expanding the functions of an existing institution in the market. Either way, the intention would be to stimulate the market for social investment, which would, in turn, lead to more enterprising, sustainable third sector organisations.

5.44 The Government is strongly attracted to boosting social investment and is keen to find ways to develop this as part of wider third sector policy over the 2007 CSR years. The Government will commit resources to boost social investment. Subject to the outcome of the current consultation on the distribution of unclaimed assets and to clarifying and addressing any state aid implications, the Government would like to see social investment as a stronger element of supporting social and economic regeneration over the coming decade. If resources permit, the Government would also like to see a proportion of unclaimed assets in England used to support social investment in third sector organisations. Responses to the consultation will be used to inform the decision making process around the best way to allocate resources for the purpose of social investment.

---

[18] The Social Investment Bank: its organisation and role in driving development of the third sector, The Commission on Unclaimed Assets, March 2007.

> **Box 5.5 Social enterprise and community ownership**
>
> Wolseley Community Economic Development Trust (Wolseley Trust) manages 2 business Parks and community facilities in the inner city area of Plymouth with a value in excess of £12 million. The two sites are provided under supportive long term lease arrangements with Plymouth City Council and in return the Trust delivers significant economic, health improvement and community development outcomes. The Trust was developed originally to provide opportunities, support and a good location for local businesses to develop in a supportive environment in order to benefit people from the former local Plymouth Wards of Ham, Stoke, Keyham and Trelawney.
>
> The Trust itself is run as a democratic and community led organisation. The Management Board consists of 9 members nominated and elected from the community, 3 Plymouth City Councillors and 3 representatives from the business community.
>
> The first Business Park in Wolseley Road opened in 1997 with 25 units and community facilities in an area of Plymouth in need of regeneration- a formerly derelict site was brought back into effective use. Since then, over 260 jobs have been supported from that formerly derelict site which was purchased by Plymouth City Council from Devon County Council, using Section 106 planning gain monies and a variety of external funding- including Plymouth Task Force, the European Union and the Single Regeneration Budget.
>
> In 1999, Wolseley Trust was invited to develop a second site nearby- a former derelict hospital site now renamed as the Scott Business Park. The Scott Business Park eventually opened for business in July 2003 and hosts a further 35 light industrial and office units which significantly increases both the local business and job creation impact and the revenue generating activities of Wolseley Trust. The site quickly became fully occupied and over 1200 jobs are supported from the Scott Business Park.
>
> The successful small and medium private businesses on site mean job creation for those living in the wards that form Wolseley Trust's catchment area, and preference is always shown to businesses demonstrating a commitment to local employment opportunities.
>
> In January 2007 Wolseley Trust celebrated 10 years of successful trading, and currently has a turnover of over £1 million from which a net operating surplus of over £189,000 a year has been generated. From that net trading surplus the Trust has been able to directly provide up to £150,000 a year for the last three years, for local community infrastructure support, including- operating the Jan Cutting Healthy Living Centre, commissioning services to help improve the health and welfare of local residents and supporting other community businesses. This project represents the biggest community driven scheme undertaken so far by Plymouth City Council and its partners and is the biggest in the South West of England.
>
> The Trust has a nationally recognised, successful track record for partnership working. It has also provided local people with the support and training they need in order to manage this significant community business.

Enabling social enterprises to work with Government

5.45   The third sector review consultation has highlighted that there is sometimes a disconnect between Government Departments' role in market making through the commissioning and procurement process and the potential contribution of social enterprise in the delivery of public policy priorities.

5.46 Social enterprises are well placed to make a valuable contribution to service delivery and to wider public policy aims and there is growing evidence both of the potential and performance of different models. In particular, social enterprises have increasingly been shown to offer opportunities to promote diversity in service delivery and provision, as well as reaching underserved markets with possible implications for changing mainstream business behaviour through demonstrating market viability.[19] They have also been seen as being able to add wider value to the economy, through providing multiple social, environmental and economic outcomes that may not be matched by mainstream competitors.

5.47 As set out in Chapter 4, the Government is also taking forward a number of measures to further recognise and support the multiple roles of third sector organisations in public service delivery, to embed best practice in the commissioning and procurement landscape and to recognise the wider value in third sector public service delivery.

5.48 The Government is committed to driving forward this agenda and of particular note for the social enterprise sector is work underway in:

- waste management, where the Waste Strategy for England identifies particular strengths of the third sector in waste prevention, re-use of goods and the pioneering work of social enterprise in kerbside collection of waste for recycling and composting.[20] The strategy sets out work to build capacity through research into the success factors behind social enterprises already active in waste and the future opportunities for the sector and plans for further support through WRAP – the Waste and Resources Action Programme;

- health and social care where the Department of Health has committed £73m over the 2007 CSR years to promote social enterprise delivery models; and,

- delivery of the 2012 Olympics where research has identified some critical opportunities for social enterprise. [21] The Department of Culture, Media and Sport will engage with the third sector to ensure that local communities are fully involved in the development of the Games, and will work to ensure that local enterprises can engage with business opportunities - a business network will alert potential providers to forthcoming work. The Office of the Third Sector is providing strategic funding to a national Olympics social enterprise partnership, led by Social Enterprise London.

5.49 Social enterprises have the potential to contribute to a range of Government Departments' strategic objectives and there is a need to further build the evidence as to where the critical opportunities exist. To support this, the Office of the Third Sector will over the 2007 CSR years support Departments to undertake market analysis and feasibility studies into areas where social enterprises could contribute further to public policy objectives. Departments will be encouraged to examine different models for social enterprise delivery in specific markets, looking at the particular benefits of social enterprise structures and the wider social, economic and environmental benefits of greater social enterprise involvement. As a first step the

---

[19] Value Led Market Driven: Social enterprise solutions to public policy goals. Andrea Westall 2001.

[20] Waste Strategy for England, Department for Environment, Food and Rural Affairs, 2007.

[21] The role of social enterprise in the London 2012 Olympic and Paralympic Games, Rocket Science UK Ltd and Social Enterprise London, March 2007.

Office of the Third Sector and the Department of Business, Enterprise and Regulatory Reform will investigate the role of social enterprise models in providing renewable energy.

Strategic voices **5.50** To enable the social enterprise sector to have a greater voice in policy making, in February 2007 the Government invited applications from social enterprise representative bodies to become strategic partners of the Office of the Third Sector. The strategic funding for the social enterprise sector is worth £3 million over the next three years. Seven new social enterprise partners were agreed in June 2007: Social Enterprise Coalition (SEC); the School for Social Entrepreneurs (with Unltd); Plunkett Foundation; Social Firms UK; Co-operatives UK; Prowess; and a national Olympics social enterprise partnership (led by Social Enterprise London in partnership with SEC).

6

SUPPORTING THE ENVIRONMENT FOR A HEALTHY THIRD SECTOR

Summary

The Government wants to improve the environment that all third sector organisations work in.

The Government will:

- ensure the regulatory environment for different types of organisation is appropriate, including by 2011 conducting a review of the operation of the Charities Act;

- work to improve financial relationships between organisations and all parts of Government, including promoting three year funding relationships. The Minister for the Third Sector will report annually to the Chief Secretary to the Treasury and the Chancellor of the Exchequer on progress on building three year funding relationships;

- continue to support and improve the one stop shop Government funding information portal;

- invest in sector support organisations to provide support to frontline groups through Capacitybuilders, backed by over £80 million;

- develop a programme of action to address skills issues raised through the third sector review consultation, including a feasibility study on setting up a Workforce Development Council for the third sector;

- create a new centre with responsibility for building evidence on the impact and nature of third sector organisations; and,

- further support the Compact, developed in 1998 as a statement of the principles of good relations between the third sector and all levels of Government.

INTRODUCTION

6.1   As set out in Chapters 2- 5 the Government recognises the vital roles that third sector organisations play in enabling voice and campaigning, building strong, active and connected communities, transforming public services and combining social, environmental and business goals. If third sector organisations are to realise their full potential as a force for good in national life in each of these areas, the environment in which they operate must allow them to thrive. The Government has a role in supporting the development of this environment, creating the conditions where third sector organisations can get established, grow and achieve their aims.

THE CONSULTATION

6.2   The interim report of the third sector review highlighted feedback from the consultation on key issues around funding and finance, partnership working, capacity building in the sector and third sector skills, including:

- short term funding (typically for one year) can lead to the diversion of valuable resources into bidding for funds. It prevents the organisation from making any medium or long term commitment to serve its users or beneficiaries and can restrict the ability of organisations to recruit, retain and invest in the best staff. Best practice in funding and contracting as set out in central guidance is not being implemented consistently; [1]

- there is a range of different "modes" of funding available. Funders should make more flexible and imaginative use of these various funding modes. Different modes are appropriate for different organisations, and for individual organisations at different points in their life cycle, according to their circumstances;

- as highlighted in Chapter 5, many third sector organisations face barriers to accessing commercial finance;

- there is strong support for the Compact within the sector and a desire for better partnership working with all levels of Government, but more is needed to make sure that its principles are consistently adhered to by the public bodies to which it applies;

- the importance of funding of effective national and local "second-tier" organisations – organisations whose principal purpose is to help frontline service delivery and campaigning groups to do their job;

- the need to further develop skills in the third sector workforce (which consists not only of employees but also of volunteers and trustees) and of the skills of public sector employees who deal with third sector organisations; and,

- many third sector organisations can show exactly what positive outcomes their work produces for their service-users or beneficiaries, or for the wider community. However, those examples are at the level of individual organisations, and there is no strong and coherent evidence base for the third sector as a whole. The consultation suggested that such an evidence base is needed, not only to promote wider public recognition of the extent and value of the sector's work but also to justify Government's increasing reliance on, and support for, the sector as a motor of social and economic regeneration.

6.3   The thematic roundtable discussion on supporting the environment for a healthy third sector highlighted the importance of the relationship between the third sector and Local Government, with the work of Local Strategic Partnerships as critical for creating an enabling environment for the local third sector. The roundtable also highlighted that there are support needs common to all third sector organisations, whatever their form or activities. Moreover, capacity building provision for the sector consists of a range of interventions at different levels of Government, including business support services. These various initiatives need to be better coordinated. There could also be specific capacity building provision to encourage and enable organisations to collaborate in the interests of efficiency. Collaboration means anything from full merger, through the forming of consortia (e.g. to tender for large contracts) to the sharing of back-office or similar services. [2]

---

[1] Improving financial relationships with the third sector: Guidance to funders and purchasers, HM Treasury, May 2006 and in Funding and Procurement, Compact Code of Good Practice, Compact, 2005.

[2] Held in Birmingham, in March 2007 and chaired by Kevin Curley of the National Association for Voluntary and Community Action.

Three year **6.4**   As a first response to the consultation, the interim report set out a commitment
funding that, when Government departments and their agencies receive their 2008-09 to 2010-11 budgets through the 2007 CSR, they will be expected to pass on the flexibility and certainty of that three year funding to third sector organisations that they fund as the norm rather than the exception. This builds on the Local Government White Paper, which set a clear expectation that Local Authorities, where appropriate will pass on three year grant funding settlements to their partner organisations.[3]

BUILDING THE ENVIRONMENT FOR A HEALTHY THIRD SECTOR

6.5   The Government recognises the critical role of the independent third sector in the key arenas set out in this report and believes that its role is to build the conditions for the sector to continue to grow and thrive.

6.6   The Government has put in place a series of measures over the last ten years to build the capacity of third sector organisations, to enable organisations to access appropriate finance and funding and to promote partnership working. Looking to the next ten years, the Government has identified five key areas where it can play a role in supporting the environment in which the third sector operates. The Government will look to ensure that:

- regulation of third sector organisations is proportionate;

- best practice in funding and financing of the third sector is followed at all levels of Government;

- Government support exists to help organisations develop their capacity to acquire and/or use resources effectively;

- evidence about the value and impact of the work of third sector organisations is generated, marshalled and disseminated; and,

- public and third sector organisations are in true partnership and strive to fulfil their undertakings to each other.

Proportionate regulation

6.7   Organisations in the third sector are independent of control by the state or by any other external agent. The Government's responsibility therefore is to ensure that the legal and regulatory environment within which they operate:

- preserves their independence;

- gives them the freedom to work in innovative ways to meet the needs of the communities they serve; and,

- sustains public confidence by providing for effective intervention when things go wrong.

6.8   The regulation that an organisation faces depends largely on three factors:

- the organisation's legal form (see Box 6.1 for the legal forms available to third sector organisations);

---

[3] Strong and prosperous communities, The Local Government White Paper, Department for Communities and Local Government, 2006.

- the organisation's status (e.g. as a charity or as a Registered Social Landlord); and/or

- the organisation's activities (e.g. employing staff; carrying out public collections; running a residential care home).

6.9 To ensure that the regulatory requirements for third sector organisations are appropriate the Government has, since the start of the third sector review:

- published a consultation document seeking views on the legislative needs of cooperatives (i.e. those established as Industrial and Provident Societies) and credit unions.[4] The long term aim is to provide the cooperative and credit union sectors with a cost-effective legislative framework, which will enable them to compete even more effectively in the economy and to continue to fulfil their valuable social role. The responses to the consultation will help to inform policy and form the evidence base for any proposed changes. HM Treasury will then prepare a full Impact Assessment of the various options for reform. The consultation closes on 12 September 2007;

- begun implementation of the accepted recommendations in the Better Regulation Task Force's report: *Better Regulation for Civil Society*;[5]

- begun implementation of the Charities Act 2006. The 2006 Act is being implemented in stages. The first stage, which was completed in February 2007, included raising the financial thresholds for registration and audit of charities; giving charity trustees new powers to help in the governance and administration of their charities; and modernising the constitution and powers of the Charity Commission. The second stage, to take place in the second half of 2007, will include provisions to make mergers between charities easier and to simplify the auditing regime for charitable companies. The third stage, to take place in early 2008, will include provisions to establish a new tribunal for challenging legal decisions made by the Charity Commission, and to establish a new legal form for charities, the Charitable Incorporated Organisation;

- announced a review of all the financial thresholds in charity law. The aim of that review will be to examine the scope for raising or simplifying existing thresholds. A consultation document will be published in autumn 2007;

- announced a review of all secondary legislation under the Charities Acts 1992 and 1993, with the aim of examining the scope for simplifying what already exists; and,

- published Departmental simplification plans for 19 Government Departments, agencies and regulators including the Charity Commission. Each plan sets out proposals for simplifying or reducing regulations for which the Department, agency or regulator is responsible. Together the plans contain over 500 measures to tackle unnecessary regulation. By 2010, these measures will reduce the overall administrative burden on business and the third sector by £2 billion.

---

[4] Review of the GB cooperative and credit union legislation: a consultation, HM Treasury, June 2007.

[5] Better Regulation for Civil Society, making lives easier for those who help others, Better Regulation Task Force, November 2005.

6.10   Taken together these measures will significantly improve the legal and regulatory environment for many third sector organisations. The Government will continue to work with the third sector to ensure that regulation remains proportionate. This will include, by 2011, a review of, and report to Parliament on, the operation of the Charities Act 2006.

Box 6.1 Organisational forms in the third sector

Some people choose to pursue their common cause or interest as an informal group of individuals. However, if they want to acquire funding from a public or third sector body; or, official recognition (e.g. registration, accreditation by a public body), they will almost always have to set up as an organisation with a recognisable legal form and a written constitution.

People wanting to set up an organisation have a wide choice of legal forms. What is most suitable will depend on the types of activities the founders want to carry out, who is to benefit from those activities, and how the organisation is to be controlled and managed.

Unincorporated forms

Charitable Trust – most commonly used by people wanting to set up a foundation which makes charitable grants but provides no services, has assets greatly exceeding any liabilities, has few contracts or employees, is governed by a small board of trustees, and has no membership.

Unincorporated association – most commonly used by people wanting to set up a membership organisation to provide a service or facilities to, or a voice for, a community. Typically, its governing committee consists of people, who are elected by, and representative of, its membership. It is likely to have few assets or liabilities and few contracts or employees.

Corporate forms

Company – most commonly used by people wanting to set up an organisation that will have large assets, a large number of commercial or public contracts to receive or deliver services, or a large number of employees. **Companies limited by shares** are found typically as wholly-owned subsidiaries of charities, set up to carry out a commercial trade that will make a profit for the charity. Where the purpose is to serve users or beneficiaries rather than to make a distributable profit the **company limited by guarantee**, which has no shareholders, is normally used. The **Community Interest Company** was created by the Government in 2004, for use by people wanting to set up a business which can be run along normal commercial lines but which has an "asset lock" to secure the application of its profits for socially useful purposes.

Charitable Incorporated Organisation (CIO) – a new corporate form created by the Charities Act 2006. Unlike the company form, which was designed for commercial activity and can be used by public, private and third sector organisations alike, the CIO was designed for, and can be used only by, charities.

Industrial and Provident Society – of which there are two types: the cooperative and the community benefit society. The cooperative is for use by people who share a common economic, social or cultural need or interest and who want to run a business together to serve that need or interest. Membership is generally open to anyone who shares that need or interest. A cooperative is controlled and run by its members for their mutual benefit. By contrast a community benefit society, while sharing the same basic constitutional structure as a cooperative, is for use by people wanting to run a business for the benefit of the community outside the society's own membership.

Best practice in funding and finance

6.11   The third sector looks to access finance from a range of sources in the public and private sectors and many in addition generate income through trading activity. Public funding of the third sector however is substantial. For the most recent year for which figures are available (2003-04):

- central Government funding was estimated at £2.8 billion (£4.9 billion including the funding of housing associations); and,

- local Government funding was estimated at £4.3 billion, (and at least £4.5 billion when the funding of housing associations is included). This gives a total for central and local Government of £7.1 billion (and in excess of £9.4 billion including the funding of housing associations). In addition to that, spending by NHS bodies on third sector organisations might have amounted to £1.6 billion in 2004-05.[6]

The funding relationship   **6.12**   The funding relationship between central Government and third sector organisations is governed by the principles set out in the Compact and its Code of Practice on Funding and Procurement, alongside HM Treasury guidance.[7] [8] Similarly, local Compacts - agreements between Local Government, local public bodies and the voluntary and community sector in their area – govern relationships at local level. 99 per cent of Local Authority areas in England are now covered by a local Compact.

6.13   In 2005, the National Audit Office examined how the funding relationship between the Government and the third sector was operating in practice. Having reviewed the NAO's conclusions the Government accepted that improvements were needed to several aspects of its funding practice:[9]

- one-year funding was conventional for some Government programmes. Moving to longer term funding, with the term determined by the objective the funding sought to achieve rather than by convention, would not only give funded organisations greater financial stability but could also prove better value for money for the Government;

- payment in arrears could cause cashflow problems for funded organisations and required them to bear alone the risk of the initial investment;

- Government funding should allow an organisation to recover the full cost to it of providing a service, including an appropriate element of its organisational overheads. The Government remains committed to the principle of full cost recovery, however a further NAO review into full cost published in June 2007 acknowledged that Departmental practice towards cost recovery will vary with the purpose of the funding and the environment it takes place in. The Office of the Third Sector and HM Treasury accept the recommendation in the report to develop more sophisticated statements on

---

[6] Office of the Third Sector estimates for funds flowing to UK third sector by grants and fees payable under contracts based on figures reported in surveys of Government departments and Local Authorities. Housing Corporation funding of Local Authority-sponsored housing association/registered social landlord schemes in England is not covered by the local government survey and is estimated separately. Indicative estimate for NHS bodies from the market mapping survey conducted by IFF for the Department of Health. The survey asked third sector organisations about their sources of funding.

[7] The Compact on Relations between the Government and the Voluntary and Community Sector in England.

[8] Improving financial relationships with the third sector: Guidance to funders and purchasers, HM Treasury, May 2006.

[9] Working with the Voluntary Sector, National Audit Office, 2005.

full cost recovery that reflect funders' responsibilities for fair treatment and risk management;[10]

- administrative processes (e.g. applications for funding, reports on the use of funds) sometimes imposed on organisations burdens which were disproportionate to the sums of money involved.

6.14 HM Treasury's *Guidance to funders* published in May 2006 provides guidance on all of these issues and makes clear that short-term funding arrangements with the third sector can create a climate of uncertainty in which long-term and sustainable planning by the sector cannot be properly considered.[11] It set out that the length of funding should be tied to the length of the objective. In the 2006 Pre-Budget Report the Chancellor of the Exchequer reiterated that when all Government Departments and their agencies receive their 2008-09 to 2010-11 budgets through the 2007 CSR, they will be expected to pass on the flexibility and certainty of that three year funding to third sector organisations that they fund as the norm rather than the exception.

6.15 **The Minister for the Third Sector will report to the Chief Secretary to the Treasury and the Chancellor of the Exchequer on an annual basis on progress in delivering the overall funding commitment for key grant programmes and contract areas. This will be based on submissions from Government Departments, who will be requested to ensure that all departures from the three years are fully justified. As part of the annual report on the Compact a regular report will be presented to Parliament on three year funding arrangements in order to encourage consistency and transparency in the process.**

6.16 This commitment recognises that sustainability in funding will reduce the incidence of organisations taking time to bid for funds, reduce burdens on public sector staff in terms of monitoring funding arrangements, encourage a more sustainable pool of providers and suppliers, support efforts towards better strategy and planning and will help to professionalise third sector organisations, allowing them to more effectively lever in other forms of finance.

Compact code on funding and procurement
6.17 As set out in paragraph 6.42, the recommended review of the Compact should include a review of the Compact Code on Funding and Procurement alongside the other Codes. The Commissioner for the Compact should consult widely within central and local Government and the third sector, in carrying out the review. **All Government Departments and their agencies over the 2007 CSR years should continue to drive improvements in funding practices overall, based on HM Treasury guidance and the Compact. All Government Departments have a responsibility for example to agree with third sector organisations how and when they are going to make payments to them, in the monitoring requirements placed upon the third sector and in acknowledging the legitimacy of the organisation being able to recover all or a proportionate amount of its legitimate overhead costs.** As set out in Chapter 4, a modernised version of Government Accounting, *Managing Public Money*, to be published in July, will include advice on working with the third sector, including issues around the recovery of appropriate overhead costs and clawback.

---

[10] Implementation of full cost recovery, National Audit Office, June 2007.

[11] Improving financial relationships with the third sector: Guidance to funders and purchasers, HM Treasury, May 2006.

6.18   The review of the Compact Code of Funding and Procurement should take account of the potential for Government to improve the effectiveness of its funding by the use of different modes:[12]

- the "giving" mode, in which the funder is typically interested in financing the continued operation of an organisation whose work it values;

- the "shopping" mode, in which the funder is typically interested in acquiring a service to a specified standard and for a specified price;

- the "investing" mode, in which the funder is typically interested in bringing about a long-term improvement in, for example, policy or in the organisation's or the sector capacity to use resources effectively; and,

- of the different forms of financial assistance – grant, contract, loan, etc – which a funder might use according to the funding mode it was adopting.

6.19   Section 70 of the Charities Act 2006 came into force in April 2007. That provision gives any Secretary of State a general power to give financial assistance, in any form, to a wide range of third sector organisations in England. Exercise of the power must be reported to Parliament annually. The Government would welcome Parliament's taking a continuing interest, perhaps through the Public Administration Select Committee, in Government funding of the third sector.

Government funding portal   **6.20**   The Government funding portal (www.governmentfunding.org.uk) was set up in September 2003 as the Government's response to a recommendation in the 2002 cross-cutting review *The Role of the Voluntary and Community Sector in Service Delivery*.[13] The purpose of the portal is to provide a single point of access to grant funding available to third sector organisations from central Government Departments (including funding provided through the Government Offices for the Regions).

6.21   The portal provides a searchable database of information about central Government grant schemes, with the facility for registered subscribers to apply online for grants. Registration is free, and the portal is popular – it currently has about 26,000 registered subscribers. However, the portal is not comprehensive even of central Government grants – only eight departments are represented, together with the nine Government Offices. The potential exists to enhance the usefulness of the portal to grant-seekers, and to build on its current popularity with subscribers. **Over the 2007 CSR years therefore, the Government will continue to invest in the running of the portal, and will consider the options for a competition to continue to provide this service. The aim will be to extend coverage initially to all central Government Departments (including Government Offices) and their sponsored Non-Departmental Public Bodies.**

Sector support and skills development

6.22   The Government has a role in providing the support for organisations to be able to access and use their resources effectively, through capacity building of organisations, skills building of individuals working and volunteering in organisations and support to promote voluntary donations by individuals to organisations.

---

12 The Grant-Making Tango: Issues for Funders, Julia Unwin, 2004.

13 The role of the Voluntary and Community Sector in Service Delivery: a Cross-Cutting Review, HM Treasury 2002.

Infrastructure support **6.23** Central Government support for infrastructure development is delivered by Capacitybuilders, a non-departmental public body established to manage the ChangeUp fund. The fund, delivered by national hubs of expertise and local consortia is targeted on helping third sector organisations access information and resources, supporting learning and development, promoting good management, leadership and employment practices and raising the profile of the sector as a place to work.

6.24 Capacitybuilders has recently conducted a comprehensive consultation on its future strategy.[14] Principal messages emerging included the need to rationalise the Changeup consortia, the desirability of re-organising a set of national services to provide advice, information and training for the local third sector and infrastructure bodies, extending the Improving Reach Programme and investing in building skills of local consortia to play a leadership role and engage effectively with Local Authorities and others. The emphasis of future plans will be on ensuring that infrastructure bodies are providing practical, tangible projects and programmes of direct benefits to the front line.

6.25 **In addition to the £5 million capital investment for Capacitybuilders, announced in Chapter 3, the Government will allocate £83 million to Capacitybuilders over the 2007 CSR years, which will support infrastructure building across the themes of the third sector review. Building on the results of both the consultation held as part of the third sector review and on the draft Capacitybuilders strategy, over the 2007 CSR years Capacitybuilders will have an increased focus on ensuring that infrastructure organisations are equipped to reach down to the smallest third sector organisations, building capacity at a community level. As set out in Chapters 2 and 5, Capacitybuilders will also invest in a voice programme and in ensuring that infrastructure is equipped to support organisations wishing to adopt a social enterprise approach.**

Skills development **6.26** The voluntary and community sector in the UK has a paid workforce of at least 608,000, equivalent to 488,000 full-time employees and amounting to 2.2 per cent of the UK's paid workforce.[15] Figures for the social enterprise sector suggest that a sub-set of enterprises (companies limited by guarantee and Industrial and Provident Societies) employ around ¾ million people – 450,000 paid employees and almost 300,000 volunteers.[16] Moreover, in England, about 11.6 million people participate in formal voluntary activity at least once a month, rising to 17.9 million who participate at least once a year.[17] Formal voluntary activity involves participation through a group or organisation. Many organisations rely on volunteers for the efficient delivery of services such as care and advice services, for income generation through fundraising and retailing, and for their governance by unpaid trustees. The skills of volunteers are therefore as important for the performance and prospects of organisations as are the skills of their paid workforce.

---

[14] Destination 2014: Investing in change, a draft for consultation, Capacitybuilders, 2006.

[15] Figures from the UK Workforce Hub, based on the 2004 Labour Force Survey.

[16] A Survey of Social Enterprises Across the UK. Research report prepared for the Small Business Service by IFF Research Ltd. July 2005.

[17] 2005 Citizenship Survey, DCLG, June 2006.

6.27 Between 1997 and 2002, a network of 80 National Training Organisations (NTOs) existed to improve skills and competitiveness across the UK economy. The Voluntary Sector NTO represented the interests of the voluntary sector in the areas of staff, volunteer and trustee training and development. In 2002, a smaller number of Sector Skills Councils (SSCs) took over the functions of NTOs. SSCs are independent, employer led organisations each with a "footprint" covering a particular industrial sector. The Government took the view that the creation of a Voluntary (or Third) Sector Skills Council was not justified, since organisations in the third sector work across a large number of industrial sectors (for example, care and development, health, creative and cultural services) and their skills needs would be met by the SSCs covering those industrial sectors.

6.28 Feedback from the consultation for the third sector review suggests however, that that has not consistently happened in practice. Although third sector organisations come within the footprints of 12 of the SSCs, in only one case (that of Skills for Care and Development) does the third sector's workforce represent any significant proportion of the overall workforce covered by the SSC. In the other cases, the third sector's workforce is too small to exert any real influence over the SSC, with the consequence, that skills needs which are specific to third sector organisations are not being met.

Leitch review **6.29** The Leitch review of skills, published in December 2006, proposes an enhanced role for reformed and relicensed SSCs, which will take the lead in developing occupational standards and in approving vocational qualifications.[18] In this context it is all the more important that third sector employers should have their voice heard on the skills needs of their paid and unpaid workforce.

6.30 The Government will take forward the actions highlighted in the Department for Education and Skills' recent third sector strategy and action plan to help develop the skills of the third sector workforce.[19] **The new Department for Innovation, Universities and Skills (DIUS) will work, in consultation with the Sector Skills Development Agency, the Office of the Third Sector, the Devolved Administrations[20] and third sector workforce representatives, to develop a programme of action to address the skills issues which have emerged through the third sector review. This will need to look ahead to the setting up of the new Commission for Employment and Skills. These actions will include a feasibility study on setting up a Workforce Development Council for the sector, which would sit within the Skills for Business Network and focus specifically on the development of skills in the third sector's paid and unpaid workforce.**

Promoting charitable giving **6.31** Voluntary donations from individuals are an important income stream for charities, representing 23.5 per cent of total income.[21] The Government has put in place a framework to encourage a broader culture of planned, regular and tax-efficient giving, including through gift aid and payroll giving. In 2000, tax reliefs for giving to charities were greatly expanded through the "Getting Britain Giving" package of measures. This included:

---

[18] Prosperity for all in the Global Economy – World Class Skills, December 2006

[19] Third Sector Strategy and Action Plan, Department for Education and Skills, July 2007.

[20] The remit of the Sector Skills Councils' runs UK wide

[21] The UK Voluntary Sector Almanac, NCVO, 2007.

- the abolition of the minimum donation limit; and,

- a new, simpler and more flexible gift aid declaration system, including ability to make an oral declaration covering a series of payments.

6.32 This was a great success for the sector. The proportion of donors using gift aid since the changes in 2000 increased from less than 1 per cent in 1999-2000 to around one third in 2005-06. The value of gift aid for charities has increased from £135 million in 1996-1997 to £828 million in 2006-2007.[22]

6.33 There is however much greater scope for charities to claim additional funds through gift aid. Budget 2007 announced that the Government would undertake a consultation to identify measures to increase take-up of gift aid and will conduct an awareness raising campaign. The consultation, launched in June 2007, is looking at a diverse range of issues such as perceived barriers amongst the general public towards gift aid; the potential of higher rate taxpayers to donate additional tax relief to charities; issues specifically affecting smaller charities; and how record-keeping and auditing processes could be improved. As part of the consultation process, a number of regional events have been scheduled over the course of August and September 2007 to engage directly with the third sector on these issues, and the Government will publish an update on the consultation at the time of the Pre-Budget report later in the year.[23]

6.34 The Government will also publish, later this year, guidance on tax efficient giving for individuals, alongside updated guidance illustrating the incentives for giving and seconding of employees by business.

Building the evidence base

6.35 Third sector organisations are active in every sphere of national life, helping to improve society for the benefit of all citizens. However the true social and economic value of their contribution is not well-evidenced or understood, for several reasons:

- even if an organisation can provide compelling evidence of the value that its own work produces, there is often no mechanism for bringing that work to wider attention as an example of innovation or good practice in its field. Thus the potential for others to emulate and build on the example is lost;

- there is no central point for the collection and dissemination of research about the sector as a whole. Potential users of such research do not know where to find it;

- there is only a small number (perhaps 100 – 150, spread across 40 or so institutions) of academic researchers seriously interested in the third sector. Despite the existence of membership bodies for researchers (e.g. the Voluntary Sector Studies Network and the Association for Research in the Voluntary and Community Sector) the third sector research community is disparate and its work is largely uncoordinated; and,

- some argue, that the sector lacks both a "research culture" – i.e. the instinct and habit of generating evidence to justify the taking of particular actions or policy positions – and an adequate research infrastructure.

---

[22] HM Revenue and Customs, April 2007.

[23] The Gift Aid consultation documents are available at www.hm-treasury.gov.uk

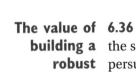
The value of building a robust evidence base

6.36 The Government believes that the building of a coherent evidence base about the sector, its organisations and their work is of paramount importance, because of the persuasive value of evidence on, particularly, those commissioning public services and those whose policies and practices third sector organisations will be campaigning to change. Chapter 4 sets out the role and priorities in building the evidence base around the delivery of public services by the third sector, while Chapter 5 acknowledges the need for more evidence of the value of social enterprise models in delivering beneficial social, environmental and economic outcomes. It is timely, therefore, that the Economic and Social Research Council (ESRC), acknowledging the increasing attention that Government at all levels is giving to the sector, has independently proposed to adopt a Third Sector Engagement Strategy, with the aim of:

- identifying needs that might be addressed through social science research, training and development, and knowledge transfer;

- establishing and promoting an evidence base of existing third sector research findings;

- building capacity and knowledge transfer opportunities within the sector; and,

- promoting the development of methodologies for evaluating the impact of social science research within the sector.

6.37 Alongside this, **the Government proposes the establishment of a new centre to take forward the important third sector research agenda. The Office of the Third Sector will invest in the setting up and running of the centre over the 2007 CSR period, and will seek to draw in further substantial funding from a range of statutory and non-statutory partners interested in third sector research. The Office of the Third Sector is already working with key partners in the development of this programme, including the ESRC and the Big Lottery Fund.**

Partnership working

6.38 The consultation showed that, within the sector, there is strong support for the Compact, and a desire for better partnership working with the bodies of Government, central and local. It also showed, however, that third sector organisations believe much still needs to be done to ensure that the Compact's principles are consistently adhered to by Government.

6.39 The principles that have been at the core of the Compact since its introduction nine years ago are sound and enduring ones. The Government remains fully committed to them as the basis for effective partnership working between Government and the third sector. The principles are set out in box 6.2.

6.40 The Government's creation in 2006 of the Commission for the Compact, and its appointment of John Stoker as the Commissioner, represents a substantial investment by Government towards the further improvement of Government/third sector partnerships. The Commission is equidistant between Government and the third sector, and acts independently of either. Its mission is to promote, through the Compact and other means, respectful and effective partnerships between Government, the rest of the public sector, and the third sector. More effective partnerships lead to greater benefits for people and communities through better policies, programmes and services. The Commission's proposed programme of work is set out in its draft business plan, published in April 2007, on which it has invited comments by 31 July 2007. **The**

Government will provide new investment for the Commission to take forward its programme of work over the 2007 CSR years. The funding allocation for the Commissioner for the Compact will be set out later in the year.

6.41 The consultation also suggested that, below the level of its enduring principles, some aspects of the Compact and its Codes were being overtaken by recent developments in policy and practice - in funding, procurement, equalities and other areas. The time is therefore right to review and refresh the Compact and its Codes, with the aim of bringing the documents fully up to date while preserving unchanged, and reaffirming, the core principles of the Compact.

6.42 The Commission's draft business plan anticipates the need for a review of the Compact. The third sector review therefore recommends that the Commission give priority to a review of the Compact. It should agree with Compact stakeholders a transparent, consultative process for the review, which should also consider how adherence to the Compact can best be assessed and reported on. It should aim to have revised Compact documentation in place in the first part of 2008-09.

Box 6.2 The Compact

The Compact on Relations between the Government and the Voluntary and Community Sector in England was published in November 1998, with the aim of creating a new type of partnership between Government and the voluntary and community sector (VCS). The Compact sets a basis for Government and the voluntary and community sector to work together to improve outcomes for the whole community:

- a healthy voluntary and community sector is part of a democratic society;

- the independence of the voluntary and community sector should be respected;

- working in partnership with the voluntary and community sector can result in better policy and services and better outcomes for the community;

- partnership requires strong relationships (e.g. integrity and openness);

- Government can play a role as funder of the voluntary and community sector.

The Government will:

- promote the Compact across Government;

- respect the independence of the voluntary and community sector;

- consult early enough to make a difference; and,

- recognise the cost of doing business when funding public service delivery.

The voluntary and community sector will:

- promote the Compact across the sector;

- operate through open and accountable organisations;

- involve all stakeholders and embrace diversity; and,

- contribute constructively to public policy.

The most recent Compact Annual Meeting (November 2006), and the third sector review consultation, concluded that the Compact was continuing to contribute strongly to the building of constructive relationships between the public sector and the VCS. There remain, however, some significant challenges for the future:

- to make the Compact relevant not just to the VCS but to the wider third sector;

- to reach a position where the principles of the Compact have become fully embedded in the culture both of central and Local Government and of the third sector; and,

- to ensure that the Compact and its Codes of Practice cater for new developments in the financial relationship between public and third sector bodies, such as payment by results and the sub-contracting out of services.

7

ENSURING DELIVERY

7.1   Chapters 2-6 set out a series of areas where the Government is committed to taking action over the 2007 CSR years, building to a joint vision of the future role of the third sector and its partnership with Government over the next ten years. The majority of actions will be led by the Office of the Third Sector in Cabinet Office. Over the 2007 CSR years, the Office of the Third Sector will invest over £515 million in third sector programmes. In addition to this, the Government will continue to match private sector contributions to the youth volunteering organisation v, to further promote a culture of volunteering and mentoring, as set out in Chapter 3.

7.2   The third sector review has been overseen by a cross-Departmental Ministerial group. To maintain progress across Government on implementation of the third sector review, this inter-Ministerial group will continue into the 2007 CSR years. The group will include Ministers from the Cabinet Office, HM Treasury, the Ministry of Justice, the Department for Environment, Food and Rural Affairs, Communities and Local Government, the Department for Children, Families and Schools, the Department for Innovation, Universities and Skills, the Department for Business, Enterprise and Regulatory Reform, the Department for Work and Pensions, the Department of Health, the Home Office and the Department for Culture, Media and Sport. The Ministerial group will report to the relevant Cabinet Sub-Committee.

7.3   The following table sets out and summarise the actions set out in the report, alongside a timetable for delivery over the 2007 CSR years.

Table 7.1 The Government's priorities for building the partnership with the third sector

Review theme	Action	Lead Department/ Agency	Key milestones
Voice and campaigning	Research to promote better understanding of effective and innovative consultation with the third sector	OTS	Scoping study in place by autumn 2007
	Capacity building support – voice, campaigning and leadership programme to enable infrastructure to provide support for frontline organisations to undertake voice and campaigning work.	OTS, Capacitybuilders	Capacitybuilders to launch three year Voice programme in April 2008
	Learning and development programmes to build understanding of how the Compact is being implemented with regard to campaigning activity	OTS, Commissioner for the Compact, CLG	Report by April 2008
	Continuation of strategic funding programme	OTS	Ongoing commitment
	Development of strategic funding programme	CLG	Subject to the outcomes of the 2007 CSR

	Support for organisations wishing to promote innovative approaches to third sector campaigning activity	OTS	Draft plans in place by April 2008
	Strengthened and rationalised third sector advisory structure	OTS	Established by April 2008
Strengthening communities	Exploration of how the contribution of local third sector organisations can be reflected in new Local Government performance framework	CLG, OTS	For the conclusion of the 2007 CSR
	Implementation of £80 million small grants programme to provide core funding to grass roots community organisations supporting community action and voice	OTS	Lead partner in place autumn 2007 and first applications to programme, spring 2008
	Implementation of £30 million Community Assets Fund		Summary of consultation responses and guidelines for programme available summer 2007
	Capital endowments to local foundations	OTS	First capital grants in place from April 2008
	Support for community anchor organisations	OTS, CLG	Funding available from April 2008
	Investment in youth volunteering – core and match funding for v	OTS	Ongoing commitment, three year funding agreement in place with v for April 2008
	Promotion of employee volunteering in the public sector	CO	From September 2007
	Goldstar, Volunteering for All, and new intergenerational programme	OTS	New combined programme announced in October 2007
	Community capacity building, increasingly focused on ensuring that infrastructure organisations able to support local community sector	OTS, Capacitybuilders	Capacitybuilders to launch new three year programmes covering: Consortia, National Support Services and Improving Reach in April 2008
	Work with Commission for the Future of Volunteering and other partners to take forward best way of enabling enhanced training for volunteers	CO	Commission to report autumn 2007

Transforming public services	Study into employment services and the third sector	OTS	In place for start of 2008
	Deliver and extend national training programme for third sector commissioners	OTS, IDeA	Training programme operational from autumn 2007. Ongoing commitment extended into 2007 CSR years
	Work to pioneer use of, and draw together leading practice in developing of, social clauses	OTS, OGC, NERCE	Ongoing
	Local surveys of the third sector, including the health of the sector in different areas and the quality of the relationships with local statutory agencies	OTS	Survey design, summer 2007. First survey undertaken by early 2009
	Opportunities for third sector involvement in public service delivery	OTS, DfT, DH, Defra, DCSF	Ongoing
	Futurebuilders capacity building programme	OTS	Futurebuilders contract re-let in January 2008
Promoting social enterprise	Awareness raising programme for social enterprise to new entrants, intermediaries and customers	OTS	New investment available from April 2008. Consultation through autumn 2007.
	Improving knowledge of social enterprise through enterprise and business studies education	OTS, DCSF, QCA	Social enterprise will be part of the secondary curriculum framework from September 2008.
	Improving the provision of business support to social enterprise through Business Link	OTS, RDAs	First tranche of funding for RDAs autumn 2007, ongoing commitment for 2007 CSR years
	Capacity building of social enterprise infrastructure, particularly where clear market failures exist	OTS, Capacitybuilders	Capacitybuilders to launch new social enterprise support programme in April 2008

	Boosting social investment	OTS/HM Treasury	Ongoing work. Consultation for distribution of unclaimed assets closes 9 August. Provisional slot for unclaimed assets legislation secured for 2007-08 session
	Market analysis support for social enterprise delivery models	OTS and OGDs[1]	Funding support available from April 2008
Supporting the environment for a healthy third sector	Implementing the commitment to three year funding	OTS and OGDs	Annual report to the Chief Secretary to the Treasury and the Chancellor of the Exchequer.
	Government funding portal	OTS	Ongoing commitment to fund an enhanced portal
	Infrastructure support, through Capacitybuilders	OTS, Capacitybuilders	Capacitybuilders to launch new three year programmes covering: Consortia, National Support Services and Improving Reach in April 2008
	Third sector skills strategy, including feasibility study into creation of new third sector skills body to focus on both paid and unpaid third sector workforce	DIUS	Skills strategy in place by April 2008
	Gift Aid consultation	HMT, HMRC, OTS	Consultation events in August and September. Consultation closes 30 September. Update in the Pre-Budget Report 2007
	New centre to take forward work to build the third sector evidence base, drawing in further co-funders	OTS, other key partners	Funding available from April 2008
	Commissioner for the Compact, and revision of the Compact Codes	OTS, Commissioner for the Compact	Consultation on the business plan ends 31 July 2007. Revised Compact documentation for first quarter of 2008-09.

[1] Other Government Departments

Printed in the UK by The Stationery Office Limited
on behalf of the Controller of Her Majesty's Stationery Office
ID5622221   07/07

Printed on Paper containing 75% recycled fibre content minimum.